CAREER PLAYBOOK:
TAKING YOUR JOB SEARCH TO THE NEXT LEVEL
SECOND EDITION

Career Coach
Dr. Peter Titlebaum

american press

60 State Street, #700
Boston, MA 02109
www.americanpresspublishers.com

ABOUT THE COVER:

As you look at the cover you will see four jerseys that have numbers on them.

#1—Networking jersey stands for the most important aspect in a job search.

#15—Resume jersey stands for the **15** seconds a potential employer looks at your resume.

#3—Interview jersey stands for the **3** stories you tell about yourself during the interview.

#24—Follow-up jersey stands for the need to send a thank you note within **24** hours after the interview.

Copyright © 2007, 2010 by American Press
ISBN 978-0-89641-480-8

Printed in the United States of America.

DEDICATION

Mom, Maxanne, who never let me quit on myself and thought all her children could reach great heights.

Dad, better known as Bernie, who wanted us to know family was the most important thing, always let us know he was proud of his children, and thought almost everything we did was "neat."

My inspiration—Garrett, Philip, and Leah, my children who help keep me grounded and never let me get a big head. It makes me smile as I think of them.

SPECIAL THANKS

This book could not have been written without the support of Debbie Meyers, Laura Greger, Courtney Hill, Leslie Marsh, Sharon Charbat, Corinne Daprano, Paul Aleskovsky, Jack O'Gorman, Lisa Warren, Amanda Kuntz, Laura McCall, Travis Roe, Corey Kaeser and Josh Studzinski and their willingness to read my many drafts.

To the students I have worked with over the years, I take great pride in watching you go after your dreams. I would not be the teacher I am if I did not get support from my students. Thanks for believing in me.

To Marci Taylor, Rebecca and Malcolm Fox from American Press, who believed in my book project!

To my teachers and coaches from Brighton High School, SUNY Brockport, The Ohio State University, and Temple University, who guided me on my path of knowledge!

To The University of Dayton, for giving me the chance to work among professionals who are dedicated to "Learn, Lead and Serve."

PREFACE

WHY THIS BOOK?

Winners at the game of life are those who learn not only from their own experiences but also the experiences of others.

What qualified me to write this book is my experience of teaching at the college level and assisting people in gaining entry into the job market. Those students who I have worked with have gained employment in the competitive world of the sports industry.

They have gained employment in the NFL, NBA, MLB, NHL, USOC, MLS, PGA, NCAA and several minor leagues. Sport is not the only area in which my students have gained success, showing that my approach works toward getting you started down the right career path.

Learning from the experiences of others allows you the opportunity to imitate ideas that have been successful and avoid other peoples' mistakes. Having over 25 years of experience in the sport management industry has given me valuable knowledge that can help you attain a job. This book grew from my desire to make the journey into the work force easier for you. I like to think of it as a playbook for picking the right career. The lessons are essential, because, like any game, you can't play well until you know the rules and strategies.

I have had the pleasure of speaking throughout the country on ways to get into the working world. Teaching others to advocate for themselves has always been my goal. It is not possible to stop people from making poor decisions; however, the purpose of this book is to guide you. The goal is to learn from your past experiences and get better at making informed decisions.

You will quickly learn that it might not be glamorous or easy, but if you have a passion for any industry, there is no reason you cannot gain employment and be successful.

This book will walk you through the steps that are essential in order for you to gain access to the world of the employed. It will supply you with valuable knowledge of the workforce and bring you closer to your dream of working in your chosen profession.

There are many ways to gain employment. Getting a job is not the goal. It's starting a career. Sit back and read how you can employ these rules. It's not as hard as those who work in the field of your choice would have you believe. This book will guide you in planning your future.

Peter Titlebaum

CONTENTS

INTRODUCTION

INTRODUCTION

This book is structured to coach you as you embark on your career path and goals. It will help you first figure out your career goals and what you want out of life, then will expand into developing materials and contacts to help you reach those goals.

TIMEOUT

Each chapter will use coaching terms to make you answer questions about yourself, your goals, and ultimately, the career you are considering. Keep in mind that life will give you "timeouts" to stop and think about your direction. Enjoy these breaks, as they will pave the way for your career journey. Thus, each chapter will have timeouts designed to guide you through effective actions you need to take to fulfill your destiny.

COACH'S TIP

This is my last point in the section before you begin. Sometimes it is not enough to just read it; I want you to understand through experience, so I may include stories from former students, my own experiences, or an additional activity for you to work through, all to help clarify the point of that particular section.

TIMEOUT HELP

I would like to thank Jim Anglin, a former MBA student who let me use personal experiences that are shared in this edition. These insights will give the reader examples of what makes a great answer to a timeout.

At the end of each chapter is a little more in-depth look at the timeouts. Many times people only answer the questions that first come to mind, so this will prompt you in reading more into questions, and looking beyond the obvious to go a step farther into true understanding and discovery. Timeout Help also serves as a short review before you move on to the next level of the book.

Everyone loves to win. My system has worked for me and others I have mentored and taught. Let me coach you toward a winning career path.

"Doc T."

Chapter One

THE RESUME GAME: PLAYING AND WINNING

GETTING STARTED: TIPS TO STAYING IN THE "IN BOX"

A resume will never get you a job. The interview will, but without the right resume, you are not going to get the interview.

Though you think your resume is outstanding and tells every potential employer that you are great, most people will never take the time to read it. The sad truth is that most employers spend less than 15 seconds looking over a resume.

This is because the business world uses resumes to disqualify people, not include them. If 200 people send in their resumes for a position, the employer must narrow the list down to less than 10. Next they will rank candidates by the resume and invite the top three in for an interview.

The goal of the resume is to keep you in the "In Box". You need to think like the future employer. This is easier than you would imagine.

Review the Given Job Description and Highlight the "True" Requirements

You will see what they are really looking for in this position. Do you possess those skills and experiences that they want? If so, you know you are on the right track, and you should put in for that position. If not, but if you have similar experience, then you should still put in for that position. However, if you don't have similar skills and experiences, the likelihood is you are wasting your time because it is not a good fit at this time.

Research

Tailor your resume to the job. While this takes more time, it is more effective in getting your resume read. The best way to do this is to look at a job description and seek out the key words. If those words are not in your resume, you will not be as effective as possible. They have a wish list in mind of what they want in a future employee, and those words are important to them.

Creative Writing

Having a resume that reads well can make all the difference in the world. So don't just throw your information in and assume the reader knows what you mean. Make it clear so they can picture your results and accomplishments.

Results

Quantify your accomplishments. You need percentages and numbers to back up your resume. If you were to look at the back of a player's baseball card, you would see his stats. That is what your resume is—your best stats—so tell how much you increased in sales, how many people participated in an event that you conducted, or the numbers of employees you supervised and trained. All those numbers will mean something to a future employer.

Proofread

Of course you will proofread your resume. I recommend taking it a step further and having people give you feedback on what they think of your resume. Look for those who you respect, those who work in the industry, and those who will be totally honest with you.

FORMATTING THE DOCUMENT

To ensure you are looked at as a possible candidate, you must have a solid layout.

Font

Keep in mind that you might want to use more than one kind of font in your resume, but don't use more than three. Using some bold fonts can make sections pop from the page. These are guidelines, and there is no set of rules. At the end of the day, you need to be happy with how your resume looks.

Email

Incorrect formatting of your e-mail address can really show your lack of attention to details.

Peter.Titlebaum@notes.udayton.edu is wrong because it shows the address as if it is a link.

It should be Peter.Titlebaum@notes.udayton.edu without the underline. If employers see it wrong on your resume, they think you are lazy and don't care about details. Worse yet, they might not be able to reach you.

Template

Find a template that assists in laying out your information. Nobody wants to look at a pile of resumes that all look alike. This is your chance to show some style, but do keep in mind that the reader needs to absorb the information in a very short period of time.

THE NO-NO LIST

I have some pet peeves that make resumes less inviting to read. STOP doing these and it will change how people look at your resume.

Colored Paper

This makes you stand out, but not for a positive reason. Please only use shades of white. Good quality paper is a nice touch.

High School Information

This is the first thing you need to take off your resume as soon as possible. Employers assume you went to high school, and they want your current information. The only way you should have something from that time in your life is if you received the Eagle Scout Award or something as noteworthy.

Objective Statement

The objective of having a resume is to get a job. There is no reason to give space on your resume for something that everyone knows before looking at it. However, you do need to put your objective in your cover letter.

Dates

A resume is like show-and-tell from grade school. You have one chance to make a positive impression. If you break experiences down into small amounts of time, you look like you might not stick with the new job very long. When listing experience, it is more effective to list the year that it took place than the specific dates.

Paragraphs

While a block of information might look impressive, put yourself in the place of the reader. The reader must inhale your information. You will be much more effective if you use bullets. When you do, keep your information to one line which is more welcoming to those reviewing it.

Two Addresses

This shows that you are a college student and living in a state of constant change. Pick the address closer to the location of the potential employer. That way, they feel better about bringing you in for an interview because most first jobs do not pay for relocation.

References

"References available upon request" is a throw-a-way line at best. The potential employer does not need this information. If they want references, they will ask. They may also contact someone they know who is not on your list because they assume that any reference will say nice things about you. Save the space for more important information.

Repeated Verbs and Tense

Those who look at resumes see many of them, and when they see one word repeated over and over again, they lose interest. The following is a list of great words that I have seen overused. Feel free to use these words, but only use them once:

Arrange
Attend
Conduct
Collaborate
Design
Organize
Plan
Manage

Do not use the following in a resume. They are not descriptive enough:

Work
Complete
Run
Help

Another rule to keep in mind is tense. When describing a current job, make sure it is in the present tense. If not a current job, make sure to use past tense.

Stating the Obvious

For some reason, many people feel the need to label every little bit of information. This is not needed, wastes space, and can make the resume seem cluttered. Examples of unnecessary labels include Address, Phone, and E-mail.

NOW WHAT?

What do you do next? You have created the perfect resume that kept you in the "inbox" and secured the job interview. Now, in order to get that job you have to know the product, yourself, inside and out. You must also perfect your sales pitch; tell the interviewer why you are perfect for the job. This book will help you do both of those. If you really think about and answer the questions posed throughout the book, you will be well on your way to closing the deal and securing that dream job.

TIMEOUT 1.1

Now that you have your resume completed it's time to see how you did. First, find a position of an available job that you would like to apply for today. Now, look at the key words found in the job description. List five words that were in the description that are not currently in your resume and find a way to include them.

This is an important step. No matter how much you personally like your resume, you need to keep in mind that those reading it are part of an industry in which you want to work. The sooner you can adapt your resume to the position you are looking for, the sooner you will find success in the job market.

Once you have added the key words to your resume, have the new and improved resume reviewed by an individual who has hired someone within this field. Ask for feedback on how your resume stacks up against other potential employees.

Report what feedback you received and then think about making changes to your current resume to reflect this feedback. Also, make a plan to gain the necessary experience to make your resume stronger.

Chapter Two

INTERVIEWING IS A POKER GAME: YOU NEED TO BE "ALL IN" IF YOU WANT TO WIN

Much has been written on how to interview. The resume may get you invited for an interview, but the interview will make or break your chances to gain employment. In other words, this is your chance to shine. Just like in a high-stakes poker game, you need to put all your chips in the center of the table and be All In! Learning to relax at this high-stakes game comes with practice and preparation, and that is what we are going to go over in this chapter.

FIRST IMPRESSIONS

First, you need to look your best. Your appearance says a great deal about you and shows your attention to detail. For instance wearing wrinkled clothes sends a bad impression. I have seen men wear white athletic socks with their dress shoes and not take the label off the sleeve of a new dress jacket; needless to say, this is not the first impression you want to make. Women should not wear open-toed shoes or a low-cut top to an interview. You want to be judged as a professional. The wrong clothes can get in the way of being taken seriously. Both genders need to be aware of using too much cologne or wearing too much jewelry. It can cut an interview short if you do not pay close attention to these details.

Other things you can control are being at least 5-10 minutes early for the interview, having a professional hand shake (that means firm but not trying to crush the other person's hand), and maintaining eye contact with the interviewer. While most people are a little nervous during the interview, failure to look at the interviewer while talking will also convey that you are unsure of yourself and your answers. This is not the impression you want to create.

RESEARCH THE COMPANY

Due diligence means doing your homework so you will be informed about the company and the position for which you are interviewing. Make sure you review the organization's web site so you have a fresh insight into the company's current business strategy. Look for upcoming projects or events. Do searches on the people you will be interviewing with, looking at their backgrounds, where they work, where they went to school, etc. While you might think this is unnecessary, these details can go a long way to develop a common thread between you and the interviewer. Prepare five "fun facts" about the organization or industry that you are interviewing. The goal would be to use at least two of these facts in the interview. If you take these steps, you will have an understanding of the company and the competition.

Examples

- When was the company founded?
- What new products have they come up with in the past years?

- What has the media been saying about them in the past six weeks?
- What new developments are going to impact the industry?
- How has the industry changed over the past five years?

Trust me when I tell you that your interviewer will be impressed that you are prepared and can have a professional conversation about their organization. It shows that you are prepared for the interview, respect their time, and that you want them to take notice of you in a positive way. All these steps show that you bring information and enthusiasm to the interview.

PREPARE FOR QUESTIONS TO ASK AND ANSWER

The interview is about control and the sharing of information. You will be asked many questions. Your first rule is to try to stay away from Yes and No answers. You need to have examples that showcase the work you have done. It is important to have percentages and numbers—an example would be managed and maintained volunteer registration system and information database for 1,150 volunteers. This kind of information would help the interviewer picture what you are trying to explain.

As you continue to read the book we will talk about creating and using a portfolio with examples of your work. This is a prop that you control, and you will need to think about how you are going to get your work into their hands during the interview. Think about one project that will showcase skills that they are looking for in a successful employee. The interview is about setting yourself apart from the crowd.

That means you need to focus on the little things, like sending a hand-written thank you note within 24 hours of the interview. This gesture shows that you really were listening and want the position. It's important to include some detail from the discussion to make you more memorable. A former student had an interview with the New York Knicks, and it happened that they were in the Lottery for the upcoming player draft. (For those non-sport fans reading this book, that means they had a bad year.)

So before the draft, he sent his thank-you note and included a lottery ticket explaining that the numbers chosen were those of retired all-time great Knicks players. The note ended saying he hoped this would bring them luck. While this type of gesture may not get you a job, it will make you stand out above the rest if everything else is equal.

As you will see in the rest of the book's samples of interview stories, you need to be as specific as possible. It is like telling them a story. While you know all the details, they are hearing it for the first time. You should be excited to share these experiences and create a movie in their mind.

The goal is to showcase your skills while interviewing, so you need to think of your stories before the interview starts. You need to make sure you don't leave the interview without telling your best stories. It's easy to say, "They did not give me a chance to share my stories," but that's your job.

EVALUATE YOURSELF AND THE EXPERIENCE

A good interview does not always land you the job, but you should consider how you really performed. Did you get your stories in and did you ask good questions of the interviewer? Did you do your homework and show case it?

Keep in mind that you are interviewing the company as much as they are interviewing you. The prospective employers perceive they have all the power of offering you a position. They do from the perspective of having the position. However, you are also evaluating the organization and those you are interviewing with at the company. There is always the time in the interview when they ask you if you have any questions of them. If you say no, you just ended the interview. While your nerves may be saying thank you for putting the painful experience behind you, you more than likely ended your shot at the position.

Interviewers expect you to ask questions, plus it is your turn to take control of the situation. It is a great chance to gain clarification on things presented earlier in the conversation. At the very least, you will want to know the time frame of the decision process. You might want to ask if you neglected to mention any critical skills they were seeking. Also, this is where I like to find out how the interviewers feel about the company. The question I like to ask is, "What is the best part about working for _____?" This gives me needed insight into what is important to the person I am interviewing. As a follow up to that question, I ask about the one thing they would like to change about the organization.

The reason for this is the interviewer should know the company or organization and this also allows you to see them lower their guard and reveal important information. It also makes them feel like you care about them and could be a good team player if offered the chance.

Evaluation starts to take place as soon as you leave the interview. I have a few questions you need to answer for yourself:

1. How did you feel the interview went?
2. What did you do that you thought went well?
3. What could you have done better?
4. Did you sell your skills, and could they see that you would be an asset to the company?

5. What phase of the interview was the easiest for you and the hardest?

6. Did the interviewer seem to like you?

7. Is there a plan for you to come back?

Most importantly, do not leave the interview without reinforcing your interest in the job. Let your interviewer see and feel your excitement about disusing the position and why you are the best fit for them.

Timeout 2.1

Interviews can be stressful—that is why you need to practice them. Your homework now is to take the job description you used in *Timeout 1.1* and find five "fun facts" related to the position, the company, or the industry in which the job is found. These facts should be information you would share during an interview for that job; facts that would impress the interviewer. Plus, you gain a sense of confidence when you have information to share during an interview.

While gathering these facts, be sure to look at the companies' web pages. They are a great source of information. You would be surprised that so many people miss this necessary step in the interview process. Don't ignore the obvious.

Chapter Three

PERSONAL INVENTORY

"You never really lose until you stop trying."
— Mike Ditka

Dream Big: Goals Often Surface

God gives us dreams a size too big so that we can grow into them.

A goal for many young people is to become an elite athlete. I remember watching the 1968 Summer Olympics and telling my mom that I wanted to compete in the Olympics. My mom, not wanting to crush my dreams, simply said, "You never know; it just might happen."

I ran track all through high school and college and was the captain of my team. However, as hard as I trained, I still was not a world-class athlete. It was time to reset my goals. I decided that if I couldn't be an elite athlete, I would coach one. So that is what I set out to do. I coached at both the high school and college levels.

The athletes and teams I worked with were able to attain great success, and I was named coach of the year for our section of the state. However this success did not lead to a full-time coaching job, and as time went by, the need to provide for a family became an important priority.

Upon reviewing my goals, I decided that returning to school was the answer. My love of sports, coaching, and teaching came together as I pursued my doctorate in Sport Management and Leisure Studies from Temple University. I am presently a college professor teaching sport management classes.

Due to hard work and my network of contacts in sports, I was fortunate to be given the opportunity to address the Olympic Congress. From that success, I was then asked to speak to Olympic athletes on how to market themselves.

Attendees at these presentations have included Olympic medalists John Naber, Leroy Burrell, and Matt Ghaffari. They came just to listen to me speak. (Mom, you were right. If you work hard, it just might happen.)

My message to you is that you never know how you might reach your goals. They may not be exactly what you had in mind from the beginning; however the important thing is to keep resetting your goals based on your values and priorities and believing in yourself, because dreams just might come true.

Timeout 3.1

Make a list of goals and a time frame for reaching them. Even if you think you may not attain each goal, you can reset your goals or come up with new goals from time to time. This will keep things challenging and will help you re-evaluate where you are in the process.

1. List 10 career goals you have for yourself/your future.
   a. Set a time frame for each goal.
   b. Map upcoming goals on a calendar.

2. Can you think of anyone that could help you achieve these goals?

Coach's Tip

As you work toward reaching your goals, get feedback from trusted sources. I had a goal of writing this book for a number of years. I was using part of it in a class, but I was having trouble finding a publisher. I sent it to a former student, Laura McCall, to review. However, Laura was concerned I would be cheating the readers if I didn't share my experiences like I do with my students who come to see me in my office. It was missing the pep talk: my coaching tips. I needed to go back and work on the book. It always helps when others believe in your goals. Thanks, Laura!

Next Year and Down the Road!

None of us believes we will be unsuccessful. If this were our mindset, there would be no need to invest our time in a book such as this. I challenge you to assess what you enjoy doing. If you were able to get paid a salary for any activity, what would you choose to do? What organizations would you be interested in working for in order to attain this type of job?

You've probably heard the expression, "Part of success is preparation on purpose." Maybe you rolled your eyes, made a gagging face, or generally blew off the saying, but it's the person who takes words of encouragement as motivation and shapes them to fit his or her ideals who ultimately will reach improbable goals.

"If you can dream it, you can do it." Lofty goals are permitted in this category. When you envision your business card of the future, what job title is directly under your name: Chief of Operations, Owner, Vice President, CEO, Coach, or maybe even a "Dr." before your name? Envisioning yourself 10 years down the road can be a useful technique when searching for direction along your career path.

Timeout 3.2

1. If you were able to get paid a salary for any activity, what would you choose?
2. List five organizations for whom you would like to work in order to attain this type of job.
3. Five, 10, or 25 years down the road, what job titles would you like to hold or have held?
4. In what ways do the jobs you listed have to do with the organizations you listed?
5. Come up with a reason why that (those) organization(s) would hire someone like you.
6. What competencies do you need to be qualified for these jobs?
7. Do you possess these competencies already, or how will you gain these skills?

Coach's Tip

There are two reasons for this Timeout. One reason is simply to focus in and choose organizations for which you would like to work.

The second reason is job titles. The reason this is important is so you can understand what skills will be required to be competitive, for example: Computer Literacy, Sales, Retail, Verbal Communication, etc. Where is the industry going, and will you have the skills to flourish? Examples: e-commerce, web page design, non-profit or profit organizations, etc. Keep in mind you need to make plans on how you will gain future skills.

Now come up with a reason why each organization would want to hire someone like you. When you come up with that answer, you can plan how to become an attractive candidate.

It's a Cinderella Story!

Your first step is to learn all you can about an industry that is most interesting to you.

Tap your heels together three times; rub a lamp and a genie appears; or your fairy godmother comes to save the day. If that's what you are waiting for to get into your dream industry, then you're in trouble. Daydreaming about going from rags to riches won't get you anywhere. So get your head out of the clouds and start doing your homework.

Your first step is to learn all you can about an aspect of the industry that is most interesting to you and aligns with your core

values. What is really important to you? What job is comple-
mentary to what you want in your life?

Searching the Internet, speaking with people whom you have
never met, and making phone calls will give you more information than you could ever have dreamed possible. Making such
calls can be hard. In sales, this is "cold calling." This means
calling a person who is not expecting the call. However, without
this information, you may only be guessing about what you need
to know and charting your course with incorrect or partial information

What people will or will not tell you often speaks volumes
about certain aspects of their industry. If they hesitate, perhaps
you need to ask for more information. If approached in a non-
threatening manner, most people will help.

Make it your goal to find out quickly if a certain career is
what you want. You may hate the first area you investigate. So
gather information quickly, and see if a particular job meets your
needs. If not, move on to the next job that interests you. This
type of approach is very efficient. It allows you to spend your
time focusing on an aspect of the industry that you really enjoy,
rather than wasting your time pursuing a job that won't hold
your interest for long.

When I was in college, I had a friend who was a Physical
Education major. She loved the classes and got great grades.
During her final semester she was required to student teach. She
hated the experience and decided she would go into sales, which
fit much better her skill and preferences.

Obtain information on many different careers so you can
make better decisions about a potential career. Don't waste years
finding out that the career you have in mind does not meet your
values and goals.

Timeout 3.3

It is not enough to just dream about your future career, you need to have a plan of action. If you know what you want to be, then you need to make sure you get all the background information you can on that particular job/industry. By doing so, you can figure out whether or not that job/industry truly is what you envision.

1. Use your list of five organizations from *Timeout 3.2*.
   a. Find the web pages for each organization.
   b. What did you learn about the organizations that you did not previously know?
2. Do they offer internships, entry level jobs, training programs, etc.?
   a. What would it take to get into each industry?
   b. Do you need to belong to a group, be an intern, etc.?

Coach's Tip

You will gain valuable information about potential careers, and maybe even some contacts, but most of all you will have a better idea about the area that suits you best. The most important part of doing your homework is getting someplace on purpose. If you were to talk to a room full of adults and ask how many have the career they intended, you would be lucky to find a few. Often they will tell you they bounced from one industry to another until they found the right job for them. So now you have a better idea of why you need to do your homework.

For the Love of the Game!

Having a passion to work in any industry is great. However, not everyone gets to work in front of the crowd.

You may love sports. However, this may not be the first thing you want to emphasize to a future employer in the sport industry.

Why not? Employers don't just want a fan. In fact, it might hurt your chances of gaining employment. A potential employer might think that all you care about is working in the sport industry because of the perceived glamour.

Being passionate is very important. However, getting a job takes more than just passion. You need experience to work in this fast paced, ever-changing industry. Being a fan is not a selling point, and it should be minimized, not maximized, as many people mistakenly do.

You wouldn't audition to be an actor just because you like to go to the movies. The sport industry is no different. Like any industry, sport is hard work, and it is not enough to just be a fan.

Every industry needs talented people in many areas. A key point to remember is that any industry you pick is a business, and a great many people want to gain entry into that field. Being creative and a problem solver will create opportunities for you to gain entry into the market of your choice.

Temper your passion by emphasizing your other talents and skills. This will make a world of difference in how your chosen industry responds to you.

Timeout 3.4

1. Assess and list your attributes. Examples: hardworking, loyal, passionate, etc. Ask yourself what it is that you bring to the table in addition to a passion for your dream industry.
2. Find out what attributes are necessary for your dream jobs listed in *Timeout 3.2* and focus on developing those. We are all passionate about something, but what do you have that is unique and how will you position this with your Dream Company?
3. What higher-level degree, i.e. Master's degree, is required to work in your chosen field?

Coach's Tip

Hard work and knowing what you want to do in life can go a long way in helping you achieve your dream job. I worked for five years as a track coach and eight years in the Jewish Community before I found my chosen field of academia. I needed a masters and a doctorate before I could gain entry. I learned a great deal from my 13 years in the work force to make me understand the price you need to be willing to pay to get where you want.

Rejection

So what if it takes you 25 tries to score that important basket? The most important thing is to keep taking shots.

Life for a basketball player is full of decisions. Imagine you are on offense and a play is called for you to run the player guarding you off a pick and then make a quick cut to the basket. You receive the perfect pass, shoot what you think is a perfect shot, then Shaquille O'Neal steps over and blocks your shot.

No points. He waves his finger at you as if to say, "Don't bring that stuff in here." You are left shaking your head and wondering what you did wrong.

A job search can be just like this. Rejection is always a part of the experience. How you handle rejection will make all the difference in the world. Evaluate your performance. It's time to be your own best friend and harshest critic. Make sure you look at the positive. What did you do particularly well? Remember your positive points, as you will want to keep them in your routine.

It's important to note the negative as well. You may also have found something out about yourself that doesn't work. This can become a positive because you can turn these weaknesses into strengths, or at least be aware of how they affect your performance. An awareness of your weaknesses can be a powerful tool.

Now go out and fail quickly! I know that sounds funny. Trust me on this point; it works. Do you think Einstein came up with his theory of relativity overnight? No. So, this time when you receive that perfect pass, put up what you think is a perfect shot. If Shaq steps over you, fake right, go left, and put the basketball up softly on the backboard. You just might score. Even though it might take you 25 tries to score, the most important thing is to keep taking shots. By making adjustments, you can achieve your goal. If you don't believe in yourself, who will? Trust in yourself, be ready for rejection, and face it directly.

Timeout 3.5

1. Have you ever been rejected? How did you deal with the rejection?
2. Did you give up, or did you improve upon your weaknesses? How?
3. List several of your weaknesses, for example: Shy, passive, not a born leader, emotional etc, and turn these weaknesses into strengths:
   a. Of your weaknesses, which can you improve upon and how?
   b. Give real life examples of how you plan to improve upon your weaknesses.
4. Of your weaknesses, which can you most likely not improve?
   a. Find a way to keep these weaknesses "out of sight," especially to a potential employer, and accentuate your strengths.
      i. *Example:* You are not a born leader, but you are very organized. So, volunteer to keep meeting minutes, organize important documents, and plan and organize the next meeting or event with dates and times.

Coach's Tip

Life for most people is full of rejection, and I am no different. However, it really depends on how you handle rejection when it comes into your life. Reframing the situation works well for me. One response could be "I've been said "no" to by better people", but that is just my way of coping with disappointment. In reality, I look at the process and see how I can get a different result the next time. I ask for as much feedback as I can get. While it might not sound nice to say so, I wish for you to fail quickly, learn what does not work, and make changes so you can get on with reaching your goal.

Ethics

If you can find those who have this quality, you will know real winners.

I took my first head-coaching job in women's track and field at Fairport High School in Rochester, NY. They were very successful before I ever got there; however, I was fortunate to have the opportunity to work with these top-notch athletes.

The season before I started working with them was a great one for Fairport. They were undefeated going into a meet between Penfield and Brockport. Penfield had not lost a track meet in their last 55 meets.

A Fairport female athlete running the 3000m felt ill, and was not able to finish that race. However, she felt better toward the end of the meet and ran in the 4×800m, which the Fairport team won. They were happy and thrilled with how the team pulled off the upset and broke Penfield's winning streak. They got on the bus and went home.

Unknowingly, they had broken a rule. They were not allowed to use a runner who was unable to complete a race earlier in the meet. Penfield did not protest until 30 minutes after the meet was over. So nothing could be done, and it was official that Fairport had won the meet.

The next day at school, the Fairport head coach, Marty Fallon, was informed of what happened. As a new coach, he was unaware of the rule. Coach Fallon met with his athletes and asked them to decide how to handle the situation. The team came back and told him they wanted to forfeit their win. While it was no fault of the girls, they did not want to win that way. It was the right thing to do, and it was a Class Act.

Timeout 3.6

1. Explain a time when you did the "right thing" that made you stand out from the crowd.
2. Are there any personal ethics you would not compromise in order to "get ahead?"
3. Remember to highlight these values as they may help you stand out in an interview.

Coach's Tip

Having a strong moral compass makes you stand out from the group. Don't be afraid to acknowledge your ethics.

Be Part of a Team!

There are many jobs that you may think are not worthy of your best effort. However, if you can handle them with professionalism, others will notice.

Every year, sports teams hold tryouts. Coaches make hard decisions regarding who to keep and who to cut. It's a lot easier to pick your top athletes than fill the last few spots on your roster.

The reason it is harder to pick the last few athletes than the stars is that these athletes will impact the team's morale. Though they won't get much playing time, they must treat practice as intensely as a game. Their job is to challenge the starters to play better and to work harder. In this important way, they help the team to sharpen their skills for winning.

These players have adjusted to their role for the betterment of the team. They take pride in playing even a few minutes of a game, even if it is the smallest job. They are the unsung heroes, and very few people understand their value and contribution to a team.

There are jobs that you may think are not worthy of your best effort. However, if you can handle them with professionalism, others will notice. When the opportunity presents itself, you will be looked at as a can-do person, someone who works hard for the team, and helps the team perform regardless of how minor it seems. So trust me, there are no unimportant jobs. You never know who is watching.

Timeout 3.7

Write about your personal favorite team experience. This does not have to involve sports per say, it's all about teamwork.

1. Write about your favorite team experience.
2. How did it feel to be part of something special?
3. What did your team accomplish, and what role did you play?
4. Look at what the job market needs and find a way to be part of the solution.
5. Examine your organizations from *Timeout 3.2* and give an example.

Coach's Tip

The goal of the internship is to get as close as you can to your dream industry. For many of my students, it can be their dream come true to work in the industry. Most important is making it a priority for you to get your money's worth out of the experience. As you start working with your supervisor, you need to ask if doing a great job will keep you in the industry.

By asking your supervisor up front for what you want to gain from the experience, you are putting your marker on the table that you are going to do a great job and will be a positive reflection on the supervisor.

In most cases, internships are not paid, and if they are, it will not be a great deal of money. You need to make sure you are getting your money's worth, which can equal the time you put into the experience.

Blue Chip

As a coach, you are lucky to get one of these athletes in a lifetime of coaching.

"Can't miss prospect." While we all might like to hear these words, very few will. I got the chance to work with a Blue Chip recruit in 1984-85. His name was Cornelius Southall, and he was a top football prospect as a running back or a safety.

Cornelius had letters from the top 50 college programs. I asked him where he planned to go to school, and Cornelius gave me his list of the top five schools that he was going to visit. It was like a Who's Who of College Football.

When I asked how long he planned on being in college, he said he was going to be in college for four years. I told him that most top college programs were set up as five-year programs. They look at athletes as investments and really don't believe that first-year student athletes are ready to compete at a top level. I recommended that he inquire about this when he went for his college visits.

Cornelius was sure I was wrong. I was only 24 at the time and just finishing my Masters in Sport Management at The Ohio State University. The last thing he wanted was to take advice from a young track coach. He did check into this on his college visits, and when he came back, he told me I was right. However, he had discovered that Notre Dame did not red-shirt their freshmen, and so he chose to go there.

I share this story because not all news is good news. Even if you don't want to hear it, it's still important to keep an open mind. Bad news can help you make important choices that will affect your career direction.

My hope is that you will find someone who will be honest with you and tell you the score before you make a mistake. While this is not always possible, it is important to try to get different points of view.

Timeout 3.8

1. Write about a time that you had your mind made up about a decision and how you gained a new perspective that changed your plans.
    a. What was that new perspective?
    b. How did it change your plans?
    c. How did it improve your plans or the end result of the plan?
    d. Who did you take advice from that helped improve this plan?
    e. What was the helpful advice?
2. List and contact five people whose perspective and advice you respect who are willing to help you evaluate your career choices. Start with your list from *Timeout 3.1,* but think of others if needed.
3. Make a promise to yourself that you will keep an open mind even when the news might be negative.

Coach's Tip

While difficult in the short run, you can make your goals come true just by keeping an open mind. Talk to others who have a different perspective from yours.

Cornelius Southall's season of learning did not end with his decision to attend Notre Dame. During track season, he was faced with yet another "change in perspective."

During the prestigious Meet of Champions, Cornelius, who was ranked as one of the top 400-meter runners in the area, was scheduled to run the 400 meters three times. He had not lost a race all season.

Cornelius was able to coast in the first race and save his energy for the next two rounds. The second race was not going to be as easy, as he drew the athlete who had the fastest time in the area.

I asked Cornelius how he was planning to run the race. He informed me he was going to run all out from the start and win the heat. I told him, "No, you are not! You are going to come in third and do enough just to get to the finals." He looked at me and said, "You are nuts! I have not lost a race this year, and you are telling me to go out and lose?"

I asked what his goal was, and he said it was to win the 400m. So who cares who wins the heat to get to the finals? Cornelius did as I suggested and kept his eye on the goal.

Cornelius Southall did win the 400m in the finals. To this day, in his position in the U.S. Secret Service, he still calls me when he wants a fresh perspective.

TIMEOUT HELP FROM REAL LIFE

This section was added in the new edition since readers had requested real examples to help them complete their timeouts. After teaching the 2008 summer MBA class on Sport Marketing I asked one of my students if I could use him as an example of the usefulness of these exercises. Thank you, Jim Anglin for sharing your way of approaching the answers.

Timeout 3.2

Salary for Any Activity

If I could be paid a salary for any activity in the world, it would be making player personnel decisions for a major league baseball team. I genuinely enjoy analyzing statistical data and making decisions based upon my analysis. Baseball, of all professional sports, is a game of statistics. I believe that I could create and execute successful statistical models to improve a team's winning percentage. This activity is similar to what I am getting paid to do in my current job with commercial foodservice equipment. While I do like performing these analyses on food equipment, I would have greater passion if my product was a major league baseball team.

Organizations of Interest

With my connection to the city of Cincinnati (born and raised) and my passion for the Reds, the obvious organization that I would want to work for is the Cincinnati Reds. By the description of my most desirable activity, I think that the natural position that I would like to achieve is General Manager. While the Reds organization is certainly my first choice, being a GM for any MLB team would be a dream come true for me.

Top Five Organizations to Work For

- *Proctor & Gamble*
- *Henny Penny (current employer)*
- *Kroger*

- *Cincinnati Reds*
- *McDonald's Corporation*

Job Titles in the Future

Five years from now, I want to hold the title of Product Development Manager. Ten years from now, I want to hold the title of Director of Marketing. Twenty-five years from now, I want to hold the title of Vice President of Sales and Marketing.

Job Organization Correlation

Kroger, P&G, and McDonald's have, in my opinion, world-class Marketing departments. Being able to attain the status of Product Development Manager, Director of Marketing, or VP of Sales and Marketing would be a phenomenal accomplishment given the size and stature of these companies. While Henny Penny's Marketing Department is nowhere close to the size or prominence of the other companies on the list, I still believe that I would be very happy with a career with them that included the three job titles mentioned above.

The Cincinnati Reds are a somewhat unique organization from the other four listed. They are unique because I do not believe that any of the job titles I've listed would be interesting to me within the Reds organization. As I mentioned above, my dream job with the Reds organization would be as a GM. In order to ascend to that level, I think that I would need to spend some time working in the scouting department and some time working in the finance department in order to hone my skills for a GM position.

Why Organizations Would Hire Me

- *P&G would hire me based upon my work ethic, detail orientation, and good communication skills. My background in Product Management would lend credibility to the claims of having the skills previously mentioned.*

- *Henny Penny has already hired me. I think that they would promote me based upon the reasons that I have listed that other companies would hire me.*

- *Kroger would hire me because of my extensive background and knowledge regarding foodservice merchandising. I have a broad perspective of what works and what does not work to drive profitability in a grocery store's deli department.*

- *The Cincinnati Reds would hire me based upon my detail orientation, good communication skills, and ability to compile and analyze data to create value. In the case of the Reds, the value I could create would be in terms of additional wins which would translate into additional revenue from ticket and vending sales, media contracts, and merchandise sales.*

- *McDonald's would hire me based upon my extensive knowledge of frying equipment. The open fryer is one of McDonald's most important pieces of equipment in their system. I understand the Engineering and Operational intricacies related to fryers. Based upon my knowledge, I could help to increase McDonald's operational efficiency which would create value to the bottom line.*

Competencies Needed for Jobs

Core competencies needed for those jobs include planning, creativity, and coordination of the many areas of Marketing including, but not limited to production, sales, advertising, promo-

tion, research and development, marketing research, purchasing, distribution, package development, and finance.

Plans to Gain Competencies

I already possess some of these competencies from my previous and current educational and work experience. I plan to gain additional focus on these competencies by completing my MBA, pursuing professional Product Management certification, and other professional certifications. I also think that my continued work experience in the area of Product Management will help to build on these competencies.

Timeout 3.8

Mind Made Up About a Decision and Changed My Mind

From the time that I was in junior high, I was encouraged by many members of my family to become an engineer. I had always excelled in areas of mathematics and science. Not having any better ideas for what I was going to pursue as a career, I followed their advice. Throughout high school I really focused on math and science classes that would prepare me for a good engineering school. I ultimately chose one of the better undergraduate engineering schools in the Mid-West and went on to get a Bachelors of Science in Mechanical Engineering.

While earning that Bachelors degree, I came to realize that engineering was not a career for which I had passion. I could adequately do the work, but I rarely enjoyed the work. At the time that I came to the startling realization that I had chosen the wrong field, I was in student loan debt for tens of thousands of dollars. I decided that a change of degrees before I finished the Bachelors of Science was a bad decision. I sat down with my co-op coordinator at my company (who is also the Vice President of Engineering) and informed him of my dilemma. He said that getting a degree in engineering was okay because it opened the door to many fields outside of engineering. *He encouraged me to finish my degree and at the same time decide which side of business I want to concentrate on—manufacturing and engineering or sales and marketing. He said that he would support me in whatever decision I made.*

I ultimately chose the sales and marketing side and began to look for opportunities within my company. The best opportunity came in 2007 when my company decided to create a department for Product Management. I did research into what Product Management was and quickly decided that I could build a career in that field. I interviewed for the position last summer and was offered the position. I began in the new department last October. Now almost eight months into my new job, every day I am thankful that I changed my mind and pursued a career in Product Management. I look forward to going to work each day and often stay late to do work, not because I have to, but because it's what I choose.

Chapter Four

BECOMING AN INSIDER

"Don't let anyone outwork you."

- Derek Jeter

Talent Scout!

Find a successful person or expert in a chosen field, and ask him/her to be your mentor.

Some people have all the luck! While playing a pick-up game in the park, a coach comes over and says, "I've been watching you and I think you have the potential to be a big-time player. With the right training, I know you could be a star. I would like to coach you. Will you let me help you?"

Hello.... it's a dream. Things rarely happen this way. You need to find a coach, not wait for one to find you. We all have had mentors and role models: parents, teachers, coaches, and employers who have cared about us to varying degrees. As you explore and learn your profession, it is wise to ask for the experienced, honest guidance of a person you trust.

When you actively seek mentors, select ones who will be interested in spending time helping you learn and perfect new skills. Tell them why you have selected them and how you believe they can assist you in your journey. Explain that you know they are busy but you wish to learn from them and then someday be a mentor yourself.

The first person you ask may not agree to be your mentor. If you are turned down, move on to the next person on your list.

Timeout 4.1

A mentor is an individual who will help you grow as a person and gain success in your life. Explain what you would like to learn from a mentor. It can be in the industry you want to work or another area in your life where you would like support.

1. Consult your list of contacts from *Timeout 3.8* for possible professional mentors, or make a list of three people to contact about mentoring you.
2. List what you would like to learn from each mentor.
3. How can each person help you learn, grow, and gain success in the future?
4. Contact one or all of these people and ask if they are willing to mentor you.
4. Explain to him/her why he/she would be a good mentor for you.

Coach's Tip

We all need guidance from time to time. There is no reason to go it alone. If you knew you could get help buying your first car from somebody who understands the industry, would you? For that matter, it could be a career, education, religion, relationships; the list is endless. So do not struggle alone; go find a mentor.

Being a Player Starts with the Mind!

Visualize achieving your goal before it ever happens.

Want to be a winner or a player in the industry? How do you get there? The answer is a lot closer than you think.

You need to believe in yourself. Most of us know that sports are 90% mental. Yes, there are those who have God-given talent, however, I refer to the rest of us as the ugly ducklings.

By that I mean there is a player in all of us just under the surface. Think of Roger Banister, the first man to break the four-minute mile. He visualized himself setting that record before it ever happened. He had broken the record hundreds of times in his mind. The only thing left was to do it on the track.

The power of the mind will help you if you are ready. If you act like a player in the industry, those around you will start to believe it. It's not easy, but it can be done. You need to train your mind to believe you are already a success.

Think, "What will it feel like when I am successful?" What will you be doing, reading, writing? Picture what your life will be like when you achieve your goal. Now you are on the path to success.

Timeout 4.2

You need to first visualize your success before you can go out and succeed, but keeping it in the forefront of your mind is also important. Plan out your success path and start thinking like a person who is in the position you want. That means you need a plan with dates and descriptions.

1. Examine your list of careers from *Timeout 3.3*, and the attributes needed from *Timeout 3.4*.

2. Imagine yourself in each career and ask: "What will it feel like when I am successful in this career?"
3. Write about what you will be doing for each career.
4. Does your dream job require a masters degree and a doctorate? In what?
5. Do you want a title attached to your name? What can you do to make it happen?

Coach's Tip

When I first started teaching, it was important to carry myself as a professional and to be thought of as a player in the industry even though I felt somewhat unsure of myself. First, I had to believe in myself and tell myself I was a player. Then I had to network, write articles, give presentations at conferences, and get quoted in the media. Every step of the way, I visualized my success. Now I look back and say I achieved what I visualized accomplishing.

If you want to be a star, you have to act that way before you get there. It really will help in the long run if you believe in yourself. Others will see your passion, and it can open doors for you; so act like you belong in the game.

Big Time Goal

Set your goal! Do your homework! Go in with your eyes wide open and don't let people tell you it cannot be done.

A former student of mine, Omar Khan, told my Introduction to Sport Management class that someday he was going to work in the NFL. Not only that, he was going to work for the New Orleans Saints. My response to him was, "That's a great goal, but don't you want to pick a better team?" Omar just smiled and said, "It has always been my dream to work for my home team, the Saints." I did not trash his dream, however, I wanted him to know what he would be coming up against.

Let's look at the statistics of such a lofty goal. There are only 1,800 players who will make it into the NFL. That means that of the hundreds of thousands of people who play college football, less than one percent will make it to the professional level.

Now consider Omar's goal: only 300 people work in front office jobs in the NFL. So if you're going to work in the NFL, you will have to be the best of the best.

This didn't discourage Omar. His response was, "OK, what do I do first?"

We developed a set of informational interview questions, and a list of 20 people in the NFL to contact, and report his results. It took him about two months. With these contacts, though, Omar had a better feel for what needed to be done. The need for college experience was stressed.

Omar volunteered with the Tulane University football team as well as at various bowl games. He made a name for himself and got an internship with the New Orleans Saints. After graduating from college in 1997, Omar got his first job in the player personnel department with the Saints, and then moved to football operations where he served as a player assistant working with player and salary negotiations.

Omar was one of only two non-lawyers to work on salary negotiations in the NFL. He wanted to be able to understand the salary cap so well that he could interpret the legalese and explain it to the front office staff. He studied it day and night until he could explain it to anyone. Being able to explain the salary cap in layman's terms was his ticket to his goal.

In 2001, Omar Khan was named Chief Negotiator for the Pittsburgh Steelers where he supervises the overall management salary cap issues and contracts.

Set your goal! Do your homework! Go in with your eyes wide open, and don't let people tell you it can't be done. Make a plan and stick with it. As you can see from Omar's story, goals are achievable.

Timeout 4.3

1. Examine your goals from *Timeout 3.1.*

    a. Break down the big goals into smaller, more attainable goals that will eventually lead to the big goal.

    b. What do you need or need to do in order to make them a reality?

    c. How would you go about approaching the goal or obtaining more information?

2. Assign potential dates to these goals, and map them out on the calendar.

Coach's Tip

Write down your goals with achievement dates. Few people have written goals, and that is why most people have not achieved them. Writing down specific goals with dates, and reviewing your list regularly keeps your dream fresh and you accountable.

Also, update your goals and timelines as appropriate. You may realize you need to volunteer or have an opportunity to intern, and your dates will need to be updated as a result.

The Inner Circle

The goal of an informational interview is to walk away with insight about a particular job or industry.

How do I get in? Is there a special handshake? Do I need a sponsor like I would if I were pledging for a fraternity or sorority? Not exactly, but if someone does take the time to show you the ropes, grab on and hold tight.

The best way to gain exposure and gather information is the informational interview process. While dreaded by many, it is actually the best way to find out exactly what a job entails. This is not an interview used to ask for a job, and that should be made clear at the onset of the interview. Nothing can discourage a contact faster then misleading them about the purpose of an interview. This is about investigating careers.

The goal of an informational interview is to walk away with insight about a particular job and/or industry.

Keep in mind that you have worked very hard to get in the door. Therefore, do not be quick to let your relationship slip away. Look for ways to keep in touch with your new contact. This may be your best chance to gain access to the inner circle.

Timeout 4.4

Refer to your list of preferred industries from **Timeout 3.3.** Meet with or call two people in the field you want to work in, and ask questions that will give you information about their positions. This information will help you decide whether or not you want these kinds of jobs.

1. Keep track of who, what company, when, contact information, etc.
2. Prepare questions before your meeting that will give you information about their positions.
3. Will you continue to stay in contact with this person in the future? Why or why not?
4. Be sure to thank each person for his/her time, following up with a handwritten note. It will make you stand out because it shows a personal style.

    a. What was written in the note? Give a summary.

    b. What creative way did you use to thank the person/ keep in future contact with him/her?
5. What did you like about the answers that you received?
6. What answers, if any, turned you off this profession or specific job?

Coach's Tip

There are two things to keep in mind:

1. Don't ask the person with whom you are having your informational interview for a job. You will lose credibility because you misled him/her on the purpose of your meeting.

2. Keep yourself connected to the person for future contact. It may be helpful to note any personal facts you have discussed (recent trips, favorite food) to comment on during your next conversation.

You have worked really hard to get inside information, and now the work really starts. You need to come up with a creative way to say thank you for the time and ask if you can stay in occasional contact with the person to keep him/her posted on your progress. Now, the kicker is, you need to do what you said you would do. Actions speak louder than words, and believe me, you worked too hard to get into the insider's door for you to close the door on yourself.

There is an art to getting back to those who interview you. A great example is a former student of mine named Laura Bartlett who had an interview with the Indiana Pacers from the National Basketball Association. After the interview, Laura sent those she interviewed a nice bowl of blue and yellow M&Ms, the team colors, and a hand-written thank-you note. They were so impressed, she got the job, because they felt if she had that kind of professional style, Laura would be the right type of person to work with their sponsors.

Giving It Away

Understand that finding a job in any industry requires prior experience.

The phrase "giving it away" is rarely a positive concept in any industry. If you give your opponent more reach or more weight in boxing, it usually is not a good thing. In football, the team with the least number of "giveaways" often wins.

You are probably wondering how "giving it away" applies to finding a job. Understand that working in any industry requires gaining prior experience. This means you selectively "give it away" by volunteering.

For example, Mike Millay wanted to work in the sports industry. Mike had a master's degree in Sport Management and started volunteering at the Young Leadership Council. The primary purpose of the organization was to bring major events to New Orleans.

The Council later became the Greater New Orleans Sports Foundation. No matter the event, Mike found a way to help, whether it was driving people to and from the airport or stuffing envelopes. He volunteered for every committee and put himself at the center of all the action. This gave him a lot of experience. Mike made himself so indispensable and valuable that when it came time to name an Executive Director for the Greater New Orleans Sports Foundation, he was their man.

Mike's experience as executive director in New Orleans made him a major player in the sports industry. The New Orleans Sports Foundation provided Millay the exposure he needed to help him attain his current position as Director of Sports Events at the Walt Disney Company.

Now I ask you, "What do you lose but your time?" Also remember that even though you are volunteering, work as hard as those who are getting paid. The trust you build may pay off long past the event.

Timeout 4.5

Once you get your foot in the door, make every opportunity count. You need to prove yourself to stay a player. Everyday, do at least one thing that you weren't asked to do. Make each day count!

1. Tell how a volunteer experience from the past has already helped you get ahead.

2. Write down an example of something you need to volunteer for and how it will help you in the job market.

   a. How will this event help you get your foot in the door of the careers you investigated in *Timeout 4.2*

   b. What can you learn from this experience?

      1) Event planning, time management, number of labor hours it takes to pull off an event, etc.

   c How will this volunteer event help you eventually get your Dream Job?

   d. What skills/attributes will you gain during this experience that will make you more valuable?

   e. How will those attributes make you more valuable?

   f. Will they help you achieve your end goal of attaining your Dream Job?

3. List several organizations that regularly need/want volunteers.

4. Pick an organization for which you would give anything to volunteer.

Coach's Tip

You already have a lot on your plate, and the last thing you want is to give away your valuable time. However, you need to look at it in one of two ways.

1. You can gain skills that will make you more valuable to your chosen industry.

2. This will also give you an opportunity to network and show an organization that you have a strong work ethic and you have what it takes to get a job done.

Perfect Practice Makes Perfect

If it were easy, everyone would be doing it!

When you get ready for competition, you need to prepare both your body and mind. There are many people trying to reach the next level. However, less than one percent, make it to professional sports.

Athletes will go out and practice a skill just to improve their game. For example, I worked with a basketball player whose right hand was dominant. I told him, "No matter what, I have your right hand covered. You'll have to use your left to get past me." After much practice he strengthened his skills with both hands, making him an invaluable addition to the team that year.

So why don't people make adjustments to their game? The answer is simple: if it was easy, everybody would be doing it. Making adjustments takes hard work and dedication. Practice or experience in the area in which you are interested will make you stronger in the long run. Identify a weakness that you would like to improve. Then find an experience that will allow you to practice and improve that skill.

Timeout 4.6

List five strengths and five weaknesses in relation to the field you wish to enter. This will give you needed insight to plan for your success.

1. List five of your strengths in relation to the field you wish to enter
2. List five of your weaknesses in relation to the field you wish to enter
3. Ask someone else to nicely tell you what is missing from your "game."
4. How can you improve upon your weaknesses?

Coach's Tip

What is missing from your game? We could all improve on some skills. Have you carefully considered what is missing from your game? Take this hard look at yourself because nobody else knows you better. Remember to ask your mentor for insight and help as well.

Batter Up

Public speaking is an important skill for your success.

Being in the on-deck circle can be a nerve-wracking experience. You're almost in the game, but there is no real pressure on you yet. No matter what the person in front of you does, the expectation is that you will be able to perform when it is your turn.

The same expectation can be said about public speaking. It is not a choice: you will be expected to have this skill, and it is one that can be learned. The audience wants you to succeed! I am not trying to say there is no stress with public speaking; however, it's an important skill for your success. The sooner you take a swing at it, the easier it's going to be when it's your turn at bat. So get some batting practice.

First, think about topics that interest you so you have some passion for the subject on which you are presenting. Keep in mind that if you've done your homework, you'll know more about your topic than your audience. If you do make a mistake, the audience will not catch it, unless you bring attention to the mistake.

Now think of places you can present your informational talks, such as clubs, schools, or public speaking groups like Toastmasters.

Timeout 4.7

The more you practice public speaking, and listen to speakers, the better your chance at success with this skill. Listen to people who you think are effective public speakers. As you listen to their presentations, take notes on their public speaking characteristics. You can also check out tips on public speaking on the internet, such as:

> http://www.school-for-champions.com/speaking.htm,

or join a group such as Toastmasters. Soon you'll develop a style that works well for you.

1. List several people you believe are effective public speakers.

    a. List the attributes that each person has that make him/her an effective speaker.

    b. Which of these attributes do you have or do you wish to gain?

    c. Prove that you have these attributes or tell how you will gain each one.

2. List what tips you always remember or use just before public speaking. Do you have a ritual?

    a. What tips helped you become a better public speaker?

3. What public speaking skills could you improve?

    a. How will you improve upon those skills?

4. List several topics about which you are passionate and on which you would feel comfortable speaking publicly.

5. Give examples from when you gave a public speech or tell when you plan to speak about a topic of interest.

Coach's Tip

The first time I taught a college class at Tulane University I was scared, but I reminded myself of some basic rules that helped:

1. Know your subject; be the expert.

2. Have passion.

3. The audience wants to be entertained.

4. Leave them with information they can use.

When You Grow Up?

A career goal has to be realistic and not just a whim.

How many times have you heard this question: "What do you want to be when you grow up?" I ask people this question all the time because if you are going to get in the 'game', you need to know certain information. For example, you say you want to be an athletic director on the Division I level. That's great, but now I start asking the hard questions.

1. Do you know any athletic directors?
2. Do you know how much they make?
3. Do you know what publications they read?
4. Do you know what conferences they attend?

This line of questioning is not meant to be cruel, but any career goal should be realistic, and research is important for every "rookie." It might put you on the spot, but if you do your homework, you will find out quickly there is a walk and talk to every industry and every job.

Once you find the answers to these questions, you may find out that the job is not what you envisioned. Maybe you don't like the number of hours athletic directors work, or you don't see yourself as a fundraiser. The job might not be what you thought it was, or you could be so pumped you can't wait to get started on the journey.

So how do you get started with the process? You start by conducting informational interviews, networking, and doing your homework so you will be prepared.

Timeout 4.8

To make sure you are going into the right field for yourself, dig deeper into the industry.

1. Examine the list of industries that you refined in **Timeout 4.4.** Use the Internet and library to find new details about these fields you did not know before.

2. Investigate the Occupational Outlook Handbook online or in the library for more information about jobs, salaries, descriptions, and projected growth of the industry.

3. Find contact information for two people working in each field, and give them a call. Ask to schedule an informational interview to find out more about their field, their job, and how they got where they are today.

4. Refer to **Timeout 4.4** for guidelines on conducting an informational interview.

Coach's Tip

Most people will have several careers in their lifetime, sometimes because this is necessary to reach an ultimate goal. Learn how to evaluate the careers you want so that you can aim more accurately for those goals.

Show Me the Money!

You can make a nice living in any industry, but it takes time.

When seeking employment in any industry, you might find yourself asking the question, "Where is the money?" Please don't enter any profession with this as your most important goal. You can make a nice living in any industry, but it takes time.

Entry-level salaries tend to be lower than what you may think you should be earning. Competition is strong in the industry, and many are willing to take a lower salary just to get their foot in the door.

Many people have become so disenchanted with their present jobs that they are attracted to a job more closely related to their hobbies. It has been said that the grass is always greener on the other side of the fence. Keep in mind that the grass still has to be mowed. Any time you make a career change, there is a learning curve. In order to make the transition into a new field, you will more than likely have to take a pay cut. That reality might keep some on the sideline; however, most people who are ready for a change from their current career are willing to take their chances.

There are people who say they love their job and that they can't see themselves doing anything else. It's great to work in an industry for which you have a passion. The goal is to look forward to going to work everyday. Life is full of choices.

Timeout 4.9

Find out the salary you can make starting out in the industry that you want to work. How much more will you be making five years down the road? It is important to have valued sources when you get this type of information.

1. Examine your list of jobs of interest from *Timeout 4.8* and research the starting salaries.
2. What will the salaries for each job be five years down the road?
3. Call a professional who holds your Dream Job and politely ask him/her to share salary information. Phrase it in such a manner that makes it clear you are interested primarily in the job, not just the money.
4. Salary information can also be found on-line.

Coach's Tip

Getting the job doesn't guarantee you a million dollar contract. Most likely, you'll start with a lower salary, so prepare yourself for living modestly, and remember to be patient. Unless you work for yourself, you will be overpaid for your first job and underpaid the rest of your life. Think of how many weeks or months you have to work before you are a contributing member in your new place of employment and you will understand why I say you are overpaid when you start your new job.

TIMEOUT HELP FROM REAL LIFE

Timeout 4.7

Effective Public Speakers and Their Attributes

I believe that the following people are effective public speakers:

- **Steve C., CEO of my company**

  Steve has confidence and relates well to all members of his audience. He has the ability to explain complex business ideas in ways that employees of all skill levels and backgrounds can understand. Steve also knows when and how much humor to introduce into his speeches to keep the crowd loose yet maintains respect. No matter the occasion, Steve always maintains a professional demeanor which also helps to secure his audience's respect.

- **Steve M., V.P. of Strategic Accounts of my company**

  I really admire Steve's ability to make each person in his audience feel like he is speaking directly to him or her. He can effectively work a crowd, and he does so with great sincerity.

- **Dick Vitale (NCAA Men's Basketball broadcaster)**

  Dick Vitale's passion for his subject matter, whether it is as a college basketball, motivational tactics, or charitable deeds, is legendary. I wouldn't say that he is an eloquent public speaker, but I don't think that his audience notices because they are so blown away by his passion. People want to believe what he is saying.

- **Bono (Lead singer of U2 and Political Activist)**
  Bono is passionate about his music and his charitable causes. He can inspire his audience using verbal and nonverbal tactics. He also masterfully wields his power and influence to persuade his audience to believe in his topic.

Topics I am Passionate About and Could Speak About Publicly

- *New product development at my company*
- *Commercial foodservice equipment energy consumption (particularly as it relates to ENERGY STAR)*
- *The importance of retirement planning and investment*
- *Cincinnati Reds*
- *The rock group U2*

Examples of Public Speaking

In June of 2007, I spoke to two groups of 60-70 about two new products in development by my company. The experience was both terrifying and exhilarating. Mastering the subject matter enabled me to speak with confidence and purpose.

The best tip that I received with regard to public speaking was to practice. I was probably a better public speaker when I was 22 years old and fresh out of college due to the practice that I got as an undergraduate. I was required by the co-op manager at my company to present twice to our senior management group each of my five years as an undergraduate. I'm sure I was horrible the first few times, but I continued to practice, and the more I presented, the better I became.

In order to improve, I need to do two things. First, I need to practice more. I will seek out opportunities in my company to speak on topics in which I am involved. Secondly, I will take notes when I am listening to an engaging speaker. I will then try to incorporate some of these traits into my own speaking style.

Which Attributes Do I Possess or Wish to Possess?

I do possess a few of these qualities. Namely, I am passionate about topics that I am familiar with and in which I believe. This is evident when I ad lib from my speaking "script" without disturbing the flow of the presentation.

Also, I gain my audience's respect by maintaining a profession demeanor during speeches. I had members of my June 2007 conference audience approach me afterward and tell me that they were impressed by my presentation.

I wish I possessed the ability to engage my audience so that all members of the audience felt like I was speaking directly to them. I think that a good starting place to improve upon with this skill is to make eye contact with members of my audience.

Pre-Speech Ritual

My pre-speech ritual always includes the following actions:

- *Frantically scribbling notes onto my PowerPoint outline (most of the time I don't use the notes during my actual presentation)*
- *I drink 6 to 12 ounces of bottled water in the time leading up to my presentation*
- *I keep a close eye on the clock so that I know how long I have to speak*

Timeout 4.9

Starting Salaries

   The starting salary for a Product/Brand Manager is approximately $60,000 as seen by the graph below (left). A Brand Manager position is a goal that I have in the three to five year time horizon. In the long-term horizon of 15 to 20 years, I would like to contribute at an executive level in a Sales and Marketing Department. The starting salary for this position is approximately $125,000, as shown on the graph below (right).

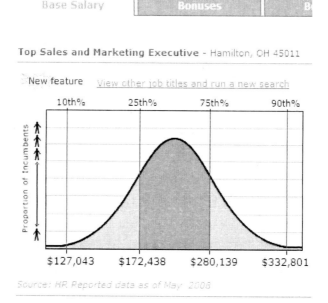

Base Salary | Bonuses | B

Top Sales and Marketing Executive - Hamilton, OH 45011

New feature   View other job titles and run a new search

| 10th% | 25th% | 75th% | 90th% |

$127,043 $172,438 $280,139 $332,801

Source: HR Reported data as of May 2008

Salary in Five Years

Five years down the road, I would imagine that I could expect to be making between the 50th and 75th percentile of income for these positions. In the case of the Product/Brand Manager, that salary should be in the range of $80,000 to $98,000. In the case of the Sales and Marketing Executive, that salary could be in the range of $225,000 to $275,000. Of course, I do not expect that I will be qualified for the executive position five years from now.

Both of these positions would be considered "good paying jobs". I was well aware of the salary implications when I accepted a position as a Product Manager last October. While a nice salary was not my main factor for entering into this field, it certainly helps to meet some of my personal goals. Ultimately, I chose the field because of my love of strategy, working with a diverse group of people, and the opportunity to be recognized at *a senior management level if I perform well. If I do well in my field, I think that the compensation will be more than enough to meet my personal financial goals.*

Chapter Five

GETTING IN THE GAME

"You have to expect things of yourself
before you can do them."
— Michael Jordan

March Madness

*The reason so few gain the employment they want is because,
just as in sports, timing is everything.*

The NCAA receives more resumes during March Madness than at any other time. The same can be said of the peak times for the Super Bowl, World Series, NBA Championships and the Olympic games.

Why share this secret? I want you to have a shot at getting a job in any industry. There are plenty of people who talk about their dream industries. One of the main reasons so few gain employment in their dream field is because, like sport, timing is crucial.

Keeping your passion alive and knowing what you can bring to the table are extremely important. There is no sense in putting obstacles in the way of that dream job, so watch your timing.

Industry doesn't need just another fan. They need people who will be part of the team behind the scenes. When times are slow, you increase your chances of getting looked at for a job.

Keep the faith, and you can make it happen. For example, do not apply for an internship *during* the Olympics, but during their "off-season" when they are not in the hustle and bustle of running the actual event.

Timeout 5.1

Whatever industry you are examining, there is a slow period of activity when fewer people are banging on the doors. This is when your job search should hit high gear.

1. For the organizations you researched in *Timeout 4.9*, when are the slow periods during when you should apply?
2. Contact your top three organizations and ask them about their "off-season."

Coach's Tip

Understanding timing is important. It is part of demonstrating that you are knowledgeable and prepared. Businesses want to hire people who have done their research and are truly interested in the industry, not just the glamour of the moment.

Midget Plays Professional Baseball

We all have certain strengths, things that we do exceedingly well, as well as things we can improve.

In 1951, Bill Veeck, owner of the St. Louis Browns, hired Ed Gadel to bat in a regulation game. Ed stood 3 feet 7 inches tall. On August 19, 1951, Gadel went up to the plate and walked on four straight pitches.

How does this apply to you? The St Louis Browns' owner never let the win/loss record of his team prevent him from bringing in fans. Veeck realized that sport is entertainment and not just winning games.

There is more than one way for a team to succeed. Attendance plays a large part of a team's bottom line. Veeck's hiring of Ed Gadel was just one of the hundreds of promotions techniques he used to get fans to attend games.

In your job search, this translates to knowing your assets and liabilities. In other words, do you know the pros and cons of what it will take for you to be successful? Use this information to your advantage. If you know your weaknesses, you can plan ahead and leverage your strengths in a variety of situations.

This is comparable to knowing your golf game. Skilled golfers think a few shots ahead. They are proactive as opposed to reactive. Plan ahead, and think of what is involved in your job search or potential career. You will be more prepared and ultimately more successful.

Timeout 5.2

Examine your list of strengths and weaknesses from *Timeout 4.6* and how you will use these in different situations. If you know how to use your strengths to your advantage, your chances of succeeding increase.

1. List your strengths.
   a. How will you use each of these in different situations? Give specific examples.
2. In the industry you wish to pursue, define "proactive."

Example: You want to be an athletic director; you must be proactive in knowing changing trends, rules, etc.

3. Call a professional in your desired field and ask that person what it means to be proactive in that job/industry.

4. List three weaknesses.

   a. Tell your strategy for turning *each weakness* into a strength.

5. Ask a peer or contact how he/she turned a weakness into a strength. Try his/her strategy.

Coach's Tip

Innovation and change can scare people. You need to get a handle on them. Whether you like it or not, the world is changing fast and so is the job market.

It is important to plan more than one way to assure your success. The job that you might have in five years may not even exist today, but you may create it by looking at the combination of your strengths, your interests, and what the market needs.

Avoid the Sand Trap

Much of what we say to one another is misunderstood. It is amazing that anything gets accomplished based on our communication skills.

Why are you having such a hard time? What is it that you don't get? Most of us have struggled with comprehending another person or making our own points understood. What is missing that causes us to have so much trouble understanding is the art of communication.

Think about what happens when you don't understand something. Do you ask for more information? Or do you think, "I must be the only one who does not understand. I will just figure it out on my own."

Many of us were taught that to ask for help is a sign of weakness. Why would we want to show a boss, co-worker, or friend that we don't understand? Because when we ask questions about a task or project, we increase our chances of success and show our interest in the topic.

Asking for help is showing your STRENGTH, not a weakness. Don't be afraid to ask for more information. It can help you avoid those sand traps.

Timeout 5.3

1. Think of three areas in which you need more information to succeed or gain a better understanding of how to do the job.
2. Identify individuals and mentors who can help you attain that information, and contact them.

Coach's Tip

We all know people who are successful. Did you ever think to ask them how they got successful? Certainly hard work was a big part but it's more than that. They worked smarter. They put themselves around other successful people. You never know, they might just help you if you are brave enough to ask.

Runners to your marks......get set....bang!

At Brighton High School, I was a sprinter. I had the good fortune to have a great coach by the name of Roy Maratta. What made him an outstanding coach was his attention to detail. The reason I bring this up is to reference a track meet in which I participated as a junior. I ran the 100 yard dash (that was back in the olden times before they called it the 100 *meters*).

Our meet was against Rush-Henrietta Sperry and would determine who would win the conference. Rush-Henrietta Sperry had a top sprinter who was one of the fastest in the area. Every point in the meet was going to be important. My older brother Andy, Brighton's best hope to win the race, was also slated to run the 100.

Andy had a slight pull in his hamstring, but Rush-Henrietta Sperry did not know about it. Though Andy considered dropping out of the race, I asked him to run anyway. It was not likely that Andy would place, but he needed to be in the race if I was going to have a shot at pulling off an upset.

I asked Andy if he would take the inside lane and I would take outside and told him that at the end of the race, the Rush-Henrietta Sperry athlete would look over at Andy's lane. When he did, I would steal the race.

Andy asked how I knew this. I told him I had seen this sprinter run before. If he had a chance to showboat he would by looking over to see Andy's position. If I was close enough, I would have a shot.

You see, Roy Maratta had us practice the little things that would make us better. In every practice we did block starts and relay handoffs so we were always ready if we had to run in the relay and dip for tape.

We also had to practice for the end of the race. In the sprints, you can win with just a lean of your chest. Too soon, and you will slow down and lose the race. Too late, and it does no good. It has to be perfect to have an impact on the race. As it turned out, the Rush-Henrietta Sperry athlete raised both his arms in victory and glanced over at Andy's lane. He never saw me win the race.

I did not win because I was better; I won because I was more prepared on the details.

Timeout 5.4

Keep in mind, even small details can make you look like a star!

1. Make a list of five things you can do that will show your attention to detail.
2. How can these make you stand out from others going for the same job?

Coach's Tip

Be a stickler for details; you never know what will make you stand out. It can be something as simple as tabs on a report or not using filler words when you speak. Keep in mind that it is up to you to make yourself a positive standout.

Plays of the Day

A professional portfolio can make a world of difference in your job search.

Fans eagerly watch the highlights from the day or week in sports. Sports television programs pick the best video clips and set them to music, so you watch just the highlights. This is great for reliving special plays or to see what was missed.

How is this related to searching for a job? An important part of the job searching game is taking the best of your best and packaging those experiences and skills into an easily accessible format.

In other words, you are creating a self-marketing or self-promotion package in the form of a portfolio. A professionally-prepared portfolio can make a world of difference in your job search. Keeping your best work in a professional binder demonstrates that you are organized and prepared.

The items to include in the binder should show a wide range: a newsletter, proposal, press release, awards, group projects, and other models of your best work. These examples of your work are also excellent public relations for your school and company. They demonstrate that you are a winner and have successfully completed a variety of projects.

An employer who is interviewing candidates for a position will be more inclined to hire the person who has taken the time and effort to prepare a visual record of his/her work.

Timeout 5.5

Make sure to save every project you create, no matter how insignificant it may seem, to help you in the job search. Start putting together your professional portfolio. It is never too early.

1. List 10 things you would like to put in your portfolio today.
2. Tell why you would include each of these.
3. What is the best piece in your portfolio?
4. Pick a job from your list of preferred careers and tell what item would best help you in an interview for that position.

Coach's Tip

It's about standing out in the interviewer's mind, and gaining control of the interview. When an interviewer asks a question, you can use a selected piece to tell a story that illustrates your attributes and show them tangible examples of what you can bring to the company.

The Basement

The goal of the internship is to get as close as you can to your dream industry. For one of my student's, Andy Arnold, it was a dream come true. He got a six month internship with the RCA Dome in Indianapolis, IN.

The staff at the RCA Dome was happy with his work, and Andy was happy with the experience. However, even if they wanted to offer him a position, he could not accept yet, because he had one more term of college left at the University of Dayton.

Once Andy graduated, he wanted to get back to the RCA Dome. Although they were happy he wanted to come back, they did not have any open positions that fit his qualifications.

A short time later, they contacted him and offered him a position in security: a position that was not even close to what he had studied and worked so hard to attain. Andy was pleased that they wanted him but never thought with all the work he put in to his degree and internship that this was going to be the best offer he would receive.

Andy came in to see me and tell me what was on the table with his job search. I told him to take the position in security, even if it was not the position he really wanted.

"Andy you'll be in that position for a short time. If you approach that job with integrity, they'll move you up." Please trust me on this one!

Five months into the job, he was bumped up, and is now one of the top people in charge of Lucas Stadium.

The moral of this story is to be willing to do well at whatever job gets you in the door in order to stand out for later positions.

Timeout 5.6

Starting at the bottom of an organization gives you nowhere to go but up! Think of the one organization you would be willing to work for in any capacity.

1. What job you be willing to do for this organization if it meant getting your foot in the door?
2. What would taking this job look like?
3. How would taking this job fit into your career plan?
4. In what ways could you leverage this position in the future?

Coach's Tip

Don't be afraid to work your way up in an organization! There are countless success stories of men and women who have made it to the top of the big leagues from small beginnings. Kim Ng, the first female to hold the position of Assistant General Manager in MLB, began her career as a project analyst with the Chicago White Sox. After years of hard work Ng is projected to be the first female GM in baseball history.

Home or Away

You have to be willing to move away to come back.

How will going away impact your life? This concept will impact where you live, the person you marry, how much money you will make, and what careers you choose for yourself.

Many years ago, I saw myself as an educator and coach. That was my dream. When I finished my masters in Sport Management from The Ohio State University, I went looking for a job in the sports industry. I was ready and was offered a job coaching track and field. You may think, "Wow, that's great. That is what you wanted to do."

Instead, I turned it down without hesitation. Although the job appealed to me, it opposed my core values. The job was in Saudi Arabia, which is not an ideal place for a nice Jewish boy.

Eight years later, after completing my doctorate, I was looking for my first college teaching job. I sat down with my family, and we set guidelines for where we were willing to move.

We decided we would go as far north as Maine, as far west as Ohio, and as far south as North Carolina. Where did I accept a job? New Orleans, Louisiana. Either I failed geography, or my core values had changed.

In fact, we decided it was more important for my teaching career to start at a school like Tulane University. Why? I will never forget what my advisor, Dr. Michael Jackson from Temple University, told me. He said, "You have to be willing to go away to come back."

I now work in Ohio, so I did get back to my values; however, I am sure I am much better off for taking the risk.

Timeout 5.7

Take a look outside your present location to areas where you would like to live, and evaluate the job markets there.

1. List three places in the world you would like to live.
   a. Find two jobs of interest in each location.
   b. Make the people holding these positions your next network contacts.
2. Evaluate the jobs and organizations on your list from *Timeout 4.9.*
   a. Research the locations where these jobs/organizations are found.
   b. Call or email your contacts there, or make new ones, and talk with them about the area.

Coach's Tip

Keep the big picture in mind. You set goals for a reason. Sometimes the best way to get there is not always a straight line. It can be hard to leave family and friends behind to achieve your goals. Sometimes there is high price you need to pay for your goals at least in the short term.

Tryout!

What happens when jobs are posted and there are hundreds of applicants for only a few openings? A well-crafted resume is your calling card to get in the door.

For the first cut, resumes are looked at for less than 15 seconds, so it's important to know how resumes are evaluated.

The people in charge of the job search are eager to reduce the volume of resumes to a workable number-a maximum of 5-10 candidates. It might seem hard to accept, but resumes *disqualify* you for most jobs. For instance, having too long a resume or an incorrect format will quickly eliminate you from the pool of candidates. The remaining resumes will be read more carefully. Hopefully, yours will make the cut, and you will stay in the inbox.

What can you do about this? Every job is set up with minimum competencies. A company wants to know that you are qualified and what experiences and skills you can bring to the table. Look at the job description listed in the ad and tailor your resume to reflect your skills in terms of the qualifications for that position.

Timeout 5.8

Have someone in your desired industry read your resume and have them tell you what they most remembered. Hopefully, it will be the aspect of your resume that is important for the job that you want.

1. Read **Introduction:** *Playing and Winning the Resume Game.*

2. Use this information to write or improve your resume.

4. Have someone you respect read your resume in 30 seconds and then tell you if what stood out is what you intended?

4. Find job descriptions of open positions in your chosen field and be sure you have or can get the qualifications for that job.

   a. Do you possess them already? How?

   b. How can you get them?

Coach's Tip

Coming up with the right words for your resume is not as hard you think. Next time you look at a job listing, look at the key words in the description, and use them to tailor your standard resume to that job application.

Rookie Shows Promise

Finding positive ways to stand out in people's minds can go a long way in helping you gain employment.

A former student of mine wanted to work in Major League Baseball. More specifically, he wanted to work for the Los Angeles Dodgers.

A lofty goal for a freshman!

The fact that he was a freshman and had very little noteworthy experience would be a handicap. I pointed out that the

Los Angeles Dodgers get thousands of resumes a year from people more qualified than a freshman in college.

Brendan decided to attend a Sport Career Conference in LA to circulate his resume. He understood that putting himself in the right place, doing the right thing, and being prepared were extremely important. Just handing out a resume and hoping for a call probably wouldn't be enough to get an interview.

We developed his personal marketing plan. It started with a business card, and on the front it said:

Sports Transaction:

Potential employer trades experience to

BRENDAN GILLMAN

In return for success to be named later.

(address and phone number)

On the back:

I deliver valuable assets:
- Enthusiasm of a rookie just trying to make the team.
- Loyalty of a die-hard fan.
- Potential of a lottery pick.
- Self-confidence of an MVP.
- Determination of a veteran trying to win his first championship!

While at the conference, he made a contact and got an internship in marketing with the Los Angeles Dodgers. The unique fact that he marketed himself on a business card put him in a position to gain an internship.

The key to being evaluated as a potential rookie is to hone in on the manager's perceived needs for the upcoming season. Insight into what the team is looking for with regard to talent will make your sales pitch easier. With this information, you will be able to demonstrate that you can make an impact on the team.

Timeout 5.9

1. Make contact with any company where you would like to work, and write down what you discovered.
2. How do you plan to be part of the solution to the company/organization goals?
3. Ask your contact or find out by research what the industry needs and how you can bring that "solution" to the table. You will be more marketable if you find out exactly what the company/organization/industry needs and how you will provide it.

Coach's Tip

In basketball, the center is considered the heart of the team. Yet on October 2, 1995, the Chicago Bulls traded away their center Will Perdue, and took a gamble on Dennis Rodman of the San Antonio Spurs, a talented but unpredictable rebounder.

Coach Phil Jackson knew no team in the NBA was going to trade the Bulls a center with starting talent like guard Michael Jordan and forward Scottie Pippen on board. So the Bulls went for the next best thing—getting rebounds. They won three straight championships as a team with no center by building on the strengths of the players they had.

The message: look at what your team needs and find a way to be part of the solution.

TIMEOUT HELP FROM REAL LIFE

Timeout 5.1

Slower Periods for Organizations I Chose

- **Procter & Gamble**

  P&G has so many global locations and manages so many unique brands that it is hard to find a time that they are in a slow period. That being said, it may be best to apply for a job at P&G based upon when other candidates are less likely to apply. Because many Americans choose to vacation during the school year's Spring Break, during the Summer, and around the Christmas holiday, those may present a good opportunity to apply for a job at P&G. Less competition should mean that your chances of landing an interview are better.

- **Henny Penny** *(current employer)*

  Henny Penny's slow period is between January and March of each year. From a Marketing standpoint, most industry trade shows take place during the months of April, May, September, October, or November. Many new product promotions and strategies are kicked off during the trade-show season. Also, equipment sales tend to pick up at the end of the year as most companies are trying to use up their capital budget before losing the unspent money.

- *Kroger*

  While Kroger does not necessarily have an off-season, it certainly does have times of the year that are busier than others. Major holidays such as Easter, Memorial Day, Independence Day, Labor Day, Thanksgiving, Christmas, and New Year's Eve are very busy times for food retailers in the US. The average consumer spends more money during the time immediately before these holidays than during non-holiday time. Therefore, it is probably best to apply for a position at Kroger between New Year's and Easter since that is the longest stretch of time between peak seasons.

- *Cincinnati Reds*

  For the Cincinnati Reds, the slow period of activity falls during baseball's off-season. Essentially the slowest time of the year is November through January. While not all activity ceases to exist in the front office when there are no games on the field, there is plenty of preparation for the following season both in terms of promotion (Reds Caravan) and in terms of talent evaluation and organizational strategy.

- *McDonald's Corporation*

  McDonald's Corporation is similar to P&G in its size and ubiquity. They don't necessarily have a slow period because people eat fast food all year long. One interesting perspective may be that the period between February and April is a bad time to apply in the Equipment Innovations group because of the Worldwide Convention held in April. Corporate employees of McDonald's are most likely very busy preparing for this event and may not have time to worry about recruitment.

Timeout 3.4

Five Things to Show Attention to Detail

1. *Time is money and therefore is a critical resource that must not be mismanaged. In order to increase the effectiveness of the new product development teams that I work with, I will develop detailed project schedules that itemize each task required for the success of the project. Since my company does not have formally trained Project Managers, these schedules are not normal operating procedure. I should be able to impress team members and managers by helping to monitor the progress of key revenue generating projects.*

2. *I will keep a weekly activity list that I will send to my manager. The weekly activity list will show my short-term, mid-term, and long-term goals and objectives. This will not only help to hold me accountable for my goals, but it will also keep my manager plugged into my progress.*

3. *A great way to show attention to detail is to write a new product specification. New product specifications are a detailed plan that engineers use when designing something. The more detail that is provided, the better chance that the final product will meet the demands of the market. With my background in Mechanical Engineering, I do an excellent job of translating market needs into a product specification.*

4. *I can take on the task of being responsible for the final design of all product control decals. Every product in my company's portfolio has a control that allows operators to adjust cooking or holding temperatures and cooking or holding times. In the past, these decals have been haphaz-*

ardly designed with no brand consistency and poor attention to detail. I can change things by bringing the art design of the decals under my control. Creating a consistent brand image and consistent functions across all product lines could improve my company's brand equity while demonstrating my attention to detail.

5. *For new product launches, I can take responsibility for launch kit design. In my business, we sell our products through distributors, so it is important to convince these distributors of the value proposition of the equipment that my company manufactures. Launch kits are the first impression that distributors get of a new product. By controlling the details of the launch kit, I can directly influence the success of new product introductions. The more successful a new product introduction, the greater revenue potential that product has for my company.*

How Attention to Detail Can Make Me Stand Out

As I have presented in each of the sections, ultimately my attention to detail can help to drive revenue for a company or it can help to impress management. In either scenario, it is a good reflection on me and the work that I do.

Chapter Six

LEARNING THE WALK AND TALK

"Attention to detail instills pride and discipline."
D. Wayne Lukas
Thoroughbred horse trainer

Like a Book

***Potential employers judge you by first impressions,
so be prepared.***

Most of us have heard the expression, "Don't judge a book
by its cover." However, this common sense rule is almost never
followed. First impressions often affect others and have an impact on a person's thought process.

Picture an attractive person across the room. You decide it
would be great to meet that person. This, however, is only the
first step. The next step is to get a better look by moving closer
to the person. Do you still feel the same way? Not sure? What
new information have you learned that might determine your
next move?

Maybe you decide that his/her hygiene is not up to your
standards or that he/she went a little heavy on the cologne. These
things might stop you dead in your tracks. If, on the other hand,
you decide he/she is attractive, it's time for the next step.

The moment of truth has arrived. The person has passed your first two tests. Your next goal is to engage him/her in a conversation. Those first few words can leave you wanting more or heading to the nearest exit. Potential employers are checking you out in the same way. They're judging you on first impressions. What can be done so that you do not make a bad first impression? This is how the game is played; now you won't be caught off guard.

Timeout 6.1

Realize that, no matter what, every interviewer will be checking you out. First impressions are very important, and appearance is a big part of that first impression. Remember this when you are getting ready for an interview. Ask people you know how they first thought of you. List what impression comes across when someone meets you for the first time. Understand these attributes, and make them work for you. Also, list three negative traits of yours and understand how to soften them to deemphasize them.

1. What can be done so that you make a good first impression?
2. List what impression comes across when someone meets you for the first time.
   a. Ask someone you just met what he/she thought of you or ask someone you know well to tell you the good and bad of what they thought of you the first time you met.
   b. Improve upon and focus on the good. Ditch the bad.
3. Get dressed in your "business" attire and have someone critique you.
   a. Critique yourself next.

4. List three negative traits of yours and consider how to minimize their impact.

Coach's Tip

Dressing for the interview may seem like child's play. However, it is not something that should be taken lightly. Not only do you need to look good, you need to look and act as if you wear those clothes all the time. If you can do that, you'll come across as a real pro.

Ready for the Big Leagues!

Your goal in the interview is to be clear, concise, and to the point.

You got the call! They want to see if you have the right stuff. It's OK to have butterflies. Most people do, even if they don't admit it. What you do to get ready at this point is crucial to increasing your chances of success.

I'm talking about the interview and how to be best prepared. Most people don't like the stress of interviews; however, this is part of the game. If you know what you're trying to sell, you are already holding some of the cards.

Your goal in the interview is to be clear, concise, and to the point. When asked questions like, "Tell me about yourself," don't ramble and give too much information. The employer is not looking for your personal life, but wants to hear what you can bring to the table.

A better way to answer this question is to give them a few words that accurately describe what they are seeking. Such words can be "hardworking," "loyal," "trustworthy," and "enthusiastic." Have examples or stories to go with your one-word descriptions, and support your stories with concrete examples from your portfolio.

Stories make the information come alive. Potential employers have already read your resume, so now they want insight into the real you as an asset to the company. Think of stories that will make you stand out in an employer's mind and give yourself a step up in entering the big leagues!

Timeout 6.2

When going into an interview, understand that you are selling yourself and that the interview process is story telling. Prepare three stories that you would want to share in an interview. Think of stories that will make your relevant attributes stand out in an employer's mind. Remember to keep them concise.

1. Prepare three stories that you would want to share in an interview.

    a. Remember to look up keywords in the job description and use those when the interviewer asks you to describe yourself.

    b. Have examples or stories to go with your descriptions.

2. Link these stories to the materials in your portfolio, or prepare new materials to show.

Coach's Tip

Even when you think you have a sound knowledge of the company or industry, and have done your research, there may be something you are missing. One key strategy when forgotten, can ruin a well laid-out game plan. You need to be prepared to ask questions too. For example:

1. Can you tell me why this position is open?
2. What do you like best about working for this organization?
3. Can you describe an "average day" for this position?
4. What is the timeline for filling this position?

Keep in mind that you are interviewing the organization as much as they are interviewing you. You may find out something that makes you change your mind about accepting an otherwise great position.

Know When to Bluff!

During an interview, one might have to do some selective answering of questions or in other words, bluffing.

Job seekers should understand why employers ask thought-provoking questions during an interview. These questions are intended to give them insight into you as a person and employee. Always be truthful, however, be careful about giving away too much information. The interviewer is looking for a certain kind of answer that will fit the profile of what he/she is looking for in company employees.

When looking for a job, one might have to do some selective answering of questions—also known as bluffing! A good example of this occurred while I was serving as an athletic director of a Jewish Community Center in Philadelphia, Pennsylvania. A student from Temple University, Ed Gershman, was interested in entering the sports industry. I made calls on his behalf and helped Ed market himself.

Ed received two job interviews for positions for which he was extremely qualified, but he was not offered either of the positions. Ed was confused as to what he was doing wrong. There was no question in my mind that he had all the necessary skills for each position. So, we went through a mock interview and reviewed his interview answers.

The question giving Ed trouble was, "What do you see yourself doing in five to seven years?" He explained that he would like to go to law school part-time.

The problem with this answer was that he never thought of how it sounded to a future employer. The employer heard that Ed was not going to be around for very long. Why would they want to invest time and money in him if he was going to leave in a few years?

Ed could have answered the question, "I see myself staying in the JCC field, and as long as I am challenged there would be no reason to leave." This would have been a safe answer and put a portion of the responsibility for his career development on the employer.

It's an appropriate answer that will not take you out of the running for a position. Ed's next interview was with the 92nd Street Y in New York City, one of the most prestigious JCC in the world. He was offered the position and accepted. Ed stayed in the position four years until he moved on to positions of greater challenge.

Timeout 6.3

Employers want to know that they can count on you to be a "top" employee. Write down three questions you want to be asked in an interview. Outline the answers you want to share with the interviewer. Be sure to include examples of why you are the best person.

1. Write down three questions you would want to be asked in an interview.
   a. Provide potential answers for each question.
2. Provide examples showing why you are the best person for this job.
   a. Pick a job and tell why, using these examples, you would be the best person for this job.
   b. Make sure you look at keywords, job descriptions, etc.

Coach's Tips

The best way to think of the interview is much like dating or picking a partner. Both parties are trying to show their best side. So be very careful in the interview process, because how you present yourself will determine whether or not your "date" calls you back.

Play What The Defense Gives You!

Your individual characteristics are your strengths;
now make them stronger!

Most people have heard a head coach make the comment,
"We played what the defense gave us." Have you ever thought
about what this really means? A team develops a certain strategy
and particular style of game because it matches its strengths.
They believe they can match the other team's strengths and make
plans accordingly.

You can do the same thing with your career. Examine your
assets, and see how they match the job market. I knew I wanted
to work in the sports industry when I started my career. I was
coaching and had just completed my masters in sport management, and I didn't think it would be difficult to get my first real
sports job. Starting my career turned out to be more difficult than
I anticipated.

I had done a skills inventory of my job strengths. What was
missing? Tangible things like alumni network or contacts,
through religious and ethnic networks.

You may be thinking, "I don't want to use those types of
things to get in the door. I want to do this based on my skills and
work experience." However, we all have different characteristics, don't be too proud or humble to use them to your benefit.
Even though it may open the door, you will still need to perform
to keep that door open.

The fact that I am Jewish helped me gain employment with
several Jewish Community Centers. I was qualified for the jobs,
but because the choice had been between two equally qualified
candidates, my religious background gave me the advantage.

Whether you are Jewish, dyslexic, Black, gay, Hispanic, male, or female, there are many employers who might look favorably on you because you bring an added dimension to the organization. Take full advantage of all opportunities when starting your career.

Timeout 6.4

You have characteristics, heritage, and associated contacts that can help you get ahead.

1. List three qualities/attributes that make you unique.
2. How can each attribute help you in the job market or your chosen industry?
3. Think about contacts associated with each characteristic that can help you get ahead. Start your list now.

Coach's Tip

I've had people tell me, "I don't want to get a job that way. I want to make it on my own. I don't need family, friends, or anything else that might make my job search easier." This is very short sighted. This is really about leveraging whatever is at your disposal. Please know that nobody gets anywhere alone. We all get help from teachers, coaches, bosses, friends, and family.

After I left the Jewish Community Center field, I was speaking at a sport industry conference. Lenny Silverman, Continental Director for JCC Maccabi Games, came up to me and said, "I can't wait to hear your presentation. I want you to know that you have already sold me." I said, "Lenny, what are you talking about?"

He went on to explain that he had seen many people leave the JCC field and they did not share that part of their work his-

tory. He was impressed I had kept it in my bio for the conference. I just told him it was part of who I am, and I am always
going to be proud of it.

Too Slow To Play!

*How you handle rejection will make a world of difference
in your life.*

"You're not fast enough to be on the team. You're too short
or too tall or not smart or pretty enough. You just don't have all
of what we're looking for. You just don't have it, Kid. Try
something else."

If you have not heard these words before at some point, you
will. How, you handle this rejection will make a world of difference in your life. No matter how good you think you are as an
athlete, there is always somebody ready to take your spot. When
that happens, what you do with that experience, and how you
handle it, can have an impact on you and your future.

When Martin Ellis and I met, this successful high school
athlete had just lost the gold medal, having fallen over the last
hurdle in the New York State summer Empire State Games. Past
success had made him complacent, and he hadn't kept his summer training up to par.

Martin was a student at a rival high school. However, I approached him shortly after the completion of the race as his head
was resting against the fence in shock and frustration. He later
told me that all he heard me say was, "Are you ready to get serious?" Martin shook off the shock of loss to ask what I meant.

While "Are you serious?" may seem like a strange question
to ask at the time, I had watched Martin run for the past few

years and knew he really had not scratched the surface of his talent. Since I coached in the area, and my athletes had some success, I offered to become his personal coach. At the time I only gave him two days to make his decision. Even at this down moment, I could see his potential. I wanted him to know he was a winner, even if he didn't think so at the time.

Two days later training started and we worked hard all that fall. By the time indoor track was over, he had already earned 10 sectional titles in his track and field career. Martin was really looking forward to spring track and adding to his total.

Life does not always go as planned. At an outdoor track invitational, he lost in both of his events. A humiliated Martin told me he was not going to run the 4 X 800 meter relay, his last race of the day. When I asked if he was hurt he said, "No, I just can't believe I lost to those guys."

I told Martin he needed to run. While we could not change what happened in those past races, this race was a fresh start. "The 800 may not be what you are known for, but it will show you can compete with the best runners, and you need to show yourself you belong with the best. While it hurts now, you might not believe this, but your best races are going to be in college. For those guys who beat you, this time may be as good as it ever gets."

Martin ran a great 800 meter and gained much needed self respect. He picked himself up from an embarrassment with a fresh perspective. As for the rest of his running career, Martin Ellis made All American in the 400-meter hurdles while running for Syracuse University.

Take control of your goals, and even if you get pushed down from time to time, if you get back up you can't help but be closer to achieving them!

Timeout 6.5

Try not to take rejection or a "no" personally. If you know you can be successful, chances are you will be regardless of how many times someone tells you "no."

1. Think of three situations in which you were rejected. Now think of at least three ways you could have or did reframe each situation to get what you wanted.
2. Practice the art of reframing questions: see how many different ways you can ask a question or approach a situation.
3. Practice this with contacts.
4. Practice this with internship interviewers.
5. Practice this with your parents.

Coach's Tip

All of us have some built-in excuse for not being successful. Learn how to maximize your strengths and minimize your weaknesses. We can all practice reframing situations. Don't let others influence what you believe about yourself.

Think about what you would do to get something if you knew you could not fail. Now apply that attitude to your job search and take some action!

The Positive of a Negative!

If you're not failing, you're not growing.

As you go through the interview process, expect to be asked to describe a situation where you failed. The interviewer is interested in hearing how you handle disappointment and what you learned about yourself.

This is a great chance to tell a story that demonstrates your ability to adapt. Please don't answer, "Wow, that's a great question," or, "I've never failed". This may be true; however, it will leave the interviewer with no understanding of how you handle a negative situation.

As an example, when an interviewer asked me this question, I told the story of running a marathon. I had finished my college career as a sprinter/middle distance runner. I wanted to continue running, so I told my college coach I wanted to run a marathon. Coach John Izzo smiled and said, "That's 26.2 miles." I said, "I know and I am going to break three hours!"

Most people set a goal to just complete that distance. I wanted more than that and had ten weeks to get ready for the Empire States Games. On the day of the race, I ran a time of three hours and one minute. I was not satisfied.

After ten more weeks of training, I ran the Skylon Marathon, which went from Buffalo, NY to Canada over the Peace Bridge. My time was three hours and two minutes. Again, I was not satisfied.

The Atlantic City Marathon was ten weeks later. I just knew I had to run. This time I set my watch alarm to go off during my run at six minutes before my self imposed sub three-hour marathon deadline.

At the 25-mile mark the alarm went off. That left me with 1.2 miles to go in less than six minutes. I told myself that it was now or never. If I wanted to make my goal, there was no holding back.

I sprinted the last 1.2 miles and crossed the line at 2:59:35. I had reached my goal. I realized what I could do if I put my mind to it.

Interviewers were pleased with my answer because the marathon story was a tangible example of my attributes. What changes have come out of your failures?

Timeout 6.6

Write about a time you faced a situation where you failed to achieve your goal. Use that story to demonstrate how you challenged yourself to succeed the next time.

1. List an experience where you failed to achieve a goal.

   a. Tell what you learned about yourself and how you might improve if what you found out happened to be a weakness.

   b. Tell how you can turn this situation into a positive. Think about "adapting."

2. Describe how you deal with disappointment. Do you dwell on it or improve upon it?

   a. Make sure any story you tell is a tangible example of your attribute(s) that you can illustrate with your portfolio.

3. How do you challenge yourself on a daily basis or in certain situations to improve upon a weakness or improve upon goal attainment?

4. Do you believe you have to fail before you succeed?

5. Have one "standout" story in mind that you believe will blow an interviewer away.

    a. Why will that story make you stand out from the crowd?

    b. What attributes did you highlight and how?

Coach's Tip

Interviews are really about telling stories. The reason for using this technique is to help those interviewing you to get to know you more easily. Also, it makes you stand out in their minds because you have shared an experience that creates a picture in their minds.

Repeat

When you find success, see if you can do it again and again.

Great teams find ways to get back into the championship game. The same can be said for the skills that you developed for your first job search. You will need to keep strengthening. One of the hardest things in the world is to follow up a great performance with one that is even better.

To stay competitive, you have to keep raising your game. There will always be somebody trying to take your place and find weaknesses in your game. Before that happens, keep evaluating your skill set and looking for ways to improve it.

The best way I have found to do this is to use a SWOT analysis. If you are not familiar with this acronym, it stands for Strength, Weakness, Opportunity and Threat. This term is used in business everyday. Whether it is a job interview, a company you would like to work for in the future, or a new project, if you take this approach, it will give you a fresh perspective. You can't help but be better prepared for whatever comes your way.

Timeout 6.7

It is time to try out this skill. Do a SWOT analysis on a company you would like to work for. This is a great start on how to be prepared for approaching a new opportunity.

1. List three strengths of the company.
2. List three weaknesses of the company.
3. List three opportunities.
4. List three threats.

Coach's Tip

Evaluating a situation or business can be overwhelming because of the sheer amount of information available. Where do you begin? The framework of the SWOT analysis allows you to focus on characteristics in a structured way.

TIMEOUT HELP FROM REAL LIFE

Timeout 6.2

Three Stories to Share During Interview

1. *I went to the highly respected GMI Engineering & Management Institute to earn my Bachelor's in Mechanical Engineering. During my time at GMI, I alternated se-*

mesters going to school and working for a foodservice equipment manufacturer. The semesters in class were grueling and I was required to average 20 credit hours for nine semesters to graduate on time. Additionally, I earned an award of distinction for my senior thesis. At graduation, I had earned a degree, written a thesis, and gained almost three years of real work experience.

2. I designed a hot food holding cabinet for a customer in Australia. The project was on an accelerated schedule, but through teamwork and constant communication, I was able to bring the project in on time and at the target unit cost. Thanks to modern technology, I was able to coordinate work taking place in Ohio, China, and Australia. The profit from this product produced a return on investment within months of its launch.

3. I became the first Product Manager at Henny Penny Corporation. Being the first person in this department came with great responsibility. I had to coordinate with other members of my team in order to create product roadmaps and vision statements for all of Henny Penny's product lines. After creating the roadmaps and visions, I had to communicate these visions back to the business in order to set the company's overall product strategy and resource allocation plan.

Describe What Interviewer is Seeking

A few powerful words to describe what an interviewer is seeking in the field of Product Management are as follows:

- Analytical
- Strategic
- Hard-working
- Team player

• *Great communicator*

These are all words that can be found in a Product Manager's job description. Each of the stories above demonstrates that I have these qualities.

Story to Make Me Stand Out

I think that the best story to make me stand out during an interview for a Product Management position is the third story that I shared above. The reason I think this is the most appropriate story is because it is relevant to the position that I worked. This story helps to demonstrate that I have all of the qualities that I described that the interviewer is seeking. It shows a tremendous amount of initiative since I was the first member of the department and was really responsible for helping to lay the groundwork for the Product Management group at my company. This story stands out versus another candidate that simply "did their job" for another company which already had a Product Management group in place.

Timeout 6.3

Three Questions I want to be Asked, and the Answers

> *Q: I see from your resume that you've only had one employer your entire career. Do you think that your limited exposure to multiple companies and industry is a detriment to you?*
>
> *A: I actually think that my long career with Henny Penny is a strength. I think that it brings to light the kind of employee I am. I am a loyal employee interested in growing with a company. During my career at Henny Penny, I have taken on different responsibilities and job titles*

which gives me a great deal of diversity when analyzing a business situation.

Q: *What is your greatest failure?*

A: *I think that my greatest failure was deciding to complete my bachelor degree in Mechanical Engineering. What I mean by that is that I realized two years into my studies that I did not want to pursue a long-term career in Engineering. I think that this story ended up with a happy ending, though. Instead of switching majors, I decided to stick it out and actually ended up doing very well while pursuing that degree. But my undergraduate degree was about more than learning about Physics and Thermodynamics; it was about learning how to problem-solve and how to make decisions. I then went on to apply those skills to the discipline of Product Management and to earning an MBA which put me in the position to be a prime candidate for the position that you are looking to fill.*

Q: *Who is your hero and why?*

A: *I have a great interest in a wide array of professional sports, so I would have to draw from pro athletes to answer this question. Tiger Woods is certainly one of my biggest heroes. I think Tiger is a great role model because even at the peak of his golf game when he was absolutely annihilating the competition, he changed his swing. He changed his swing! Why in the world would the best golfer in the world be inclined to change something so fundamental to his success? When asked that, Tiger's answered, "I wanted to be better." I hope to be able to emulate that mentality in my own career. I don't want to rest on my successes. Rather I want to strive to new levels.*

Why I Am the Best Candidate for Product Manager Position

Attributes of a Product Manager include planning and coordination of production, sales, advertising, promotion, research and development, marketing research, purchasing, distribution, package development, and finance. That being said, I am the best candidate for this Product Manager position because of my hard work, my attention to detail, and my communication skills.

A good example of my hard work attribute is the fact that I am the first person to arrive at the office most mornings and I am often one of the last to leave the office each evening. While many people in my office are surfing the internet at lunch time, I am doing work for an MBA class, catching up on work, or networking with managers in my company.

A good example of attention to detail is the fact that I've managed two new product development projects which requires a high level of detail orientation. Constructing and maintaining a project schedule to guide a cross functional team toward a new product launch requires attention to detail, diligence, and coordination.

And finally, an example of my exemplary communication skills is the time that I was chosen to give a presentation to approximately 65 people during my company's distributor conference. While that doesn't sound all that extraordinary, I should mention that I gave this presentation with only three day notice after joining my company's Marketing Department.

Chapter Seven

LIFE IS IN THE DETAILS

"You gotta believe."
Tug McGraw

MVP to Benchwarmer

You can't rest on your past accomplishments.
Savor these experiences and build on them.

It's great to be the star player, the best of the best. However, success creates new pressures. Bernie Titlebaum, my father, explained this to me.

Shortly after high school graduation, my father began taking down the trophies, plaques, and awards that I had won during my high school days in track and field. Since I was the youngest in the family and the last to go off to college, the bookshelves were packed with my awards.

They had been in the family room, which might seem tacky to an outsider. However, our family was very proud of each child's accomplishments. He carefully put them in a box and in the closet in my bedroom.

When I asked him what he was doing, my father said, "Peter, you did so many great things in high school, and you should be very proud of yourself. However, you are opening the next chapter in your life. It's time to start over and set new goals to win new awards. If you ever doubt yourself, you can always go back and look in the box and know you have the right stuff to be successful."

Keep in mind you can't rest on your past accomplishments. Take pride in the journey; truly experience what you are going through while you are in the throes of battle. Savor these experiences and build on them.

Don't think you are finished learning. If you do, others will succeed at your expense. The only person you truly need to compete with is yourself. Keep setting the bar higher. You will win more awards than you ever dreamed possible.

Timeout 7.1

Don't ever think that you've accomplished everything. Once you slow down, someone else is there to either take your position or take your dream job. What stars are you shooting for?

1. Review your list of goals and the timeline from *Timeouts 4.2* and *4.3*.

    a. Update and refine the goals and needed steps for anything that is left on your list.

2. Brainstorm and dream about new goals.

    a. If you had to leave your job, what would you want to do?

    b. If you could move, where would you go?

    c. What goals have you left undone?

3. What have you learned about goal-setting and planning?

Coach's Tip

Always strive for something new. Review your goals and timeline regularly to keep yourself accountable, but also to have something to attain.

Building a Championship Team

When striving to be your best, do not be satisfied with just winning it all. Maintaining the success that you strive for is the name of the game.

The New York Yankees have won the World Series 26 times. Some fans love to hate the Yankees and complain that their success is due to the fact that they are a large market team.

The Yankees have always had owners who spend lots of money. Yet, if you think about the Chicago Cubs, you realize spending money does not guarantee championship teams. They are a large market team but have not won a World Series since 1908.

It takes more than just money to maintain success. Just ask Rupert Murdoch who bought the Los Angles Dodgers for $570 million in 1998. He had one of the highest payrolls in all of baseball, yet the Dodgers have not won a World Series since 1988. In fact, they have won a total of five World Series in the 100 plus years of their existence.

When striving to be your best, don't be satisfied with just winning it all. Maintaining the success that you strive for is the name of the game.

The Yankees continue to be a championship team because they are always on the lookout for the best and newest talent. The way they accomplish this is through networking.

Each one of us knows approximately 300 people. How often one communicates with these people varies. However, if you were to ask a CEO how many people he is in regular communication with, the answer would be 1,000 plus.

What is it that these CEOs know that someone just entering the industry doesn't? Many times success is not only who you know, but who knows who you know.

In other words, if you know 300 people, don't you think there are some people on that list willing to help you? Some may even have a contact in the industry that you want to work in and, if not, one of their contacts might.

It's about having faith in the law of numbers. If you keep working at anything long enough, it will happen. If you are satisfied easily, you may win once or twice. However, in the long haul, you won't be able to stay at the top. Networking is the blueprint for your success even after you have won your first championship or landed your first dream job. The need for networking never ends.

Timeout 7.2

Make sure that you stay in some form of contact with the people you know, because you never know when you may need to call on them.

1. List three professional contacts with whom you want to renew contact.

2. What will the next step be for each one?

3. Right now, think of all the people you know. One of them must know someone who works in sports. Call that per-

son and use the person to whom they refer you for your next contact.

Coach's Tip

"I swing big with everything I've got. I hit big or miss big. I like to live as big as I can."

– Babe Ruth

The moral of the story is that you need to keep networking, and it is OK if it does not work out every time. You need to keep at it.

Dynasty

One of the most difficult things in sports is to be considered a dynasty. When thinking of classic dynasties, most would think of the Yankees, Celtics, Packers, and Canadians. In today's fast-paced world, where money plays an even bigger role, it is harder to put long winning streaks together. The dynasty has been somewhat redefined in our modern society. Today, winning two championships in a row can be considered a dynasty.

The dynasty concept is important because most likely you will be doing something to make money from the time that you are a young teen to the time you retire, and some of us may never be able to retire, due to the not saving for retirement or just a bad economy. When things are going well, you need to think about how to make it last.

I have boiled this down to four words: Planning, Risk, Crisis, and Evaluation. This tool will stop you from becoming too complacent with a good performance. We forget to be critical when things are going well. We all like accolades for doing a great job. However, what won last year might not win the next year.

Timeout 7.3

Choose a risk you want to evaluate for your future, i.e. taking a job 10 hours from home. Come up with at least five items for each stage: Planning, Risk, Crisis, and Evaluation.

1. What risk would your Dream Job require you to take?
   Would you be willing to take that risk?
   Examples: Moving away from home.
   Taking a position outside your field to get your foot in the door.

2. What crises might happen because of taking this risk? This is something over which you don't have control. It is totally out of your hands when lighting strikes or a company goes out of business. You need to think of the worst thing that could happen and make a plan for it.

3. You moved from Ohio to California to work for your dream company. There was an earthquake that caused the organization to relocate and downsize and as a result, you lost your job.
   a. What would your next step be?
   b. How would you deal with this "backfire" to your risk?

4. Evaluate the impact that your choice could have on your career and life.

Coach's Tip

The one thing that some people and organizations avoid is evaluation. Most can't wait to move on once the event is over, and dread rehashing mistakes, but evaluation allows you to mine the experience for the good as well as the bad. Find the gems in the situation and start the process again: PLAN to improve it!

One of My Heroes

To set yourself apart from the rest of the field, think outside the box. Come up with creative ideas that solve potential employers' problems.

Many sport fans and historians know the name Dick Fosbury and his accomplishments. Fosbury won the gold in the high jump in the 1968 Olympics. Winning the gold medal did not make him a hero to me. It was the way he solved a problem that was so impressive. Dick represents for me the power of thinking outside the box.

High jump rules stated that you must jump off one foot when approaching the bar. The rest of the world was doing the Western Roll, which was a way of getting over the bar.

Fosbury came up with a new way of jumping over the bar. He created what became known as the Fosbury Flop. Instead of going over with his feet or one of his legs first, he went over the bar with the back of his head first.

The Fosbury Flop looked different. People laughed and made fun of Dick, however he stayed his course and now the whole world uses the Fosbury Flop to high jump. Dick Fosbury made his name known to the rest of the world because he knew how to think outside the box.

Timeout 7.4

1. List two things you could approach in a new/different style that might be more effective than the way you have been taught in the past.

    a. Example: Event planning: How could you improve the event for next time?

2. Tell precisely how you will improve on each of these to make them more effective.

3. Have you already made an adjustment to an event/ style/situation that helped to revolutionize the way of thinking about that certain event/style/situation?

    a. Use this story for your portfolio or in an interview.

Coach's Tip

Don't be afraid to push the envelope and try new ways to solve problems. You might just come upon something that could help you become a star.

Playing the Right Zone

Be willing to take risks in order to get ahead in your field. Sometimes you will succeed and sometimes you will not but every risk NOT TAKEN is a potential opportunity missed.

Zone defense can be an effective strategy to win games. Each player is responsible for playing a certain area of the court, and nothing else. If you play the zone correctly, your team can win the game. However, most professional teams don't play that way. Each player develops skills so that they can play any part of the court or game as needed, making them more versatile and the team more effective overall.

Many people like to play it safe. They feel comfortable, confident, and knowledgeable in their own little corner of the business. If you can get out of your "comfort zone," great things can happen.

Volunteer for an organization or event. You will find that the contacts you make can open a door down the road. You can write an article and get your name noticed. You can hone your public speaking by giving a presentation at a conference. Put yourself in a leadership role, and don't just sit on the sidelines.

It's time to push away your fears. Think outside the box. Go beyond one-dimensional thinking. You need to tell yourself "I am a player," take action, and get out of your "comfort zone." No one else can do this for you.

Timeout 7.5

What is your "comfort zone" and come up with three obstacles that you are facing and look for ways to improve your comfort level and grow as a person.

1. Explain what makes you uncomfortable
2. What are three ways you can improve and grow as a person?
   a. Make an action plan for yourself with the steps need for you to feel more comfortable.
   b. Put into words, how it will feel not having these obstacles in your life.

   Examples: Volunteer for an organization or event and find that the contacts you make can open a door down the road. Write an article and get your name noticed. Hone your public speaking by giving a presentation at a conference. Put yourself in a leadership role; don't just sit on the sidelines.

Coach's Tip

Back when I was trying to make a name for myself, I had an idea for a story. I was giving a presentation at a conference and there was a woman from *USA Today* who was speaking. After her talk, I pitched my story idea. She thought the idea had some merit and gave me a name of another contact at the paper. A few weeks later, I was published in *USA Today*.

It's time to get out of your "comfort zone" and start taking educated risks. Like most people public speaking was hard for me. While those who know me today may find this hard to believe I was scared to get up in talk in front of people. However if I was going to move forward in my career, I need to get over this obstacle. If you really want to gain employment in your dream industry, you have to take chances.

Over/Under

*Learn to be ready for change because it is coming
whether you are ready or not.*

Betting on the "Over/Under" is a term used by odds makers
and sports enthusiasts who wager on games. Let's say there's a
football game between the Buffalo Bills and the New York
Giants. The line (total number of points scored by both teams)
for the game is 43 points. A person betting on the game has a gut
feeling that it will be a defensive battle and bets that the total
points scored by both teams will be less than 43.

What does this have to do with a job? You may be overpaid
for your first job and underpaid the rest of your life. How can
that be true? The first person to hire you spends a great deal of
time and money training you for the job. For this reason, many
employers believe employees are overpaid when they start a new
job because of the learning process they must undergo. It may
take several weeks or even months to make a significant contribution to the company.

Today, people average between five and seven careers
throughout a lifetime. People are no longer satisfied staying with
one company for a lifetime. Although there are exceptions,
staying in one position is not the rule. Learn to be ready for
change. Oftentimes the longer you stay with a company, the
more they will treat you just well enough to keep you coming
back. Most companies want you to feel comfortable with your
current lifestyle so you will stay even if you could make more
money somewhere else. There is more to life than a big salary,
and that's what companies are betting on.

The only way to avoid this trap is to realize that you are your
own company. Make up your mind to view yourself as self-em-

ployed. This will assist you in being in control as a decision maker.

Timeout 7.6

Being ready for change means anticipating the next step from where you are right now. If you had to move on to a new job tomorrow, are you ready?

1. List and define five of your strengths. Listing these will help you better understand their value to an employer.
2. Tell a story proving each strength.

Coach's Tip

Learn to take stock of your skill sets. You are more than the company that you work for in today's society. Take care not to get fat and lazy; life can change in moments. Just ask the people who worked for Enron. While it is nice when things are going well, are you ready when they are not?

Chris Sprague, who worked for the Columbus Blue Jackets during the last strike, was a former student of mine. I called him during that time and asked if he had updated his resume. He said, "No." I told him to get me a copy, and I would help him update it. A few days after we made the changes to his resume, a contact asked him for his resume, and he was ready. Now Chris is the assistant to the League President of the International Baseball League.

Coach Gets schooled!

Even if you are good at your job, you are not done learning!

I was fortunate to be hired at the age of 22 as Head Track and Field Coach at Fairport High School located in upstate New York near Rochester. The Athletic Director at the school was Dave Martens. Dave was one of the top in his field, not just in New York, but in the United States.

Like most people my age, I was pretty sure I knew it all. As a coach, I believed I put in more hours and that my athletes were ready for anything the sport had to offer. We had a great deal of success (16-0) over two years with two sectional champion teams.

However, one of the most valuable lessons I learned through my coaching experience was away from the track. Having coached the top team, the media was eager to interview me about them. It opened the door for me to share why my team was successful. When the article hit the news stands, I was pretty pleased.

The next day, when I checked in at the office to get my mail, I was told that the Athletic Director wanted to meet with me. Seasoned coaches who had worked for many years did not want to be summoned to his office. I was thinking that it was a positive article about the team, so what could be so bad?

I went to meet with Dave Martens who was sitting behind his desk with the article front and center before him. He started by saying, "Nice article." He continued with, "BUT while everything you said in the article was true, it was very short-sighted." I asked what he meant. He pointed out that in the article I mentioned things that I was doing for my athletes. However, had I ever considered what others might think when they read the article?

Dave Martens pointed out that saying, 'We" rather than "I" was a more powerful and supportive way to phrase it. "We at Fairport High School" carries more weight than "I." Besides, nobody gets anywhere by himself. So share the glory, and you will impact more people than you will ever know.

Timeout 7.7

Most of us have heard the phrase, "There is no I in team." Do we really understand the lesson that is being taught?

1. Think about a time that you took credit for something you did, and you were proud of that accomplishment. You were in your glory. Now realize that somebody supported you.

2. If you could do it over again, how would you share that moment? People will appreciate the gesture and will feel part of the success.

Coach's Tip

I am thankful for getting this lesson early in my career. It has made me a better teacher, mentor, and friend. It is very satisfying to include others in my work and make sure they get the recognition they so richly deserve. So I did learn the lesson that "no man is an island," and you can't get anywhere without the support of others.

Protect the Goal

Always remember to take notes when you are in a meeting. This will help you remember what went on, and it will help when other people have questions about the meeting.

There are many ways to move up the corporate ladder. Be a good offensive player and you will succeed. Never forget the term CYA. It means "Cover Your Assets." It is imperative that you learn to develop a paper trail and have records. Many times people say one thing and do another. Some people truly forget, and others are looking out for their own best interests.

A successful strategy I have used is to follow up a conversation with a letter or email clarifying a conversation to make sure I didn't misunderstand the message. This simple yet effective strategy assures those with whom you deal that you take notes, that you are ready for anything, and that you know how to protect your goal.

Timeout 7.8

1. Develop an email that you could send a boss or co-worker that would be a CYA for a project.
2. Have a contact test your e-mail. Ask them if you properly understood what they told you.

Coach's Tip

Be a can-do person. Many times you will be put in a position where you have a group project. The last thing you want to do is take the leadership position because you might get stuck doing most of the work. However, a good leader manages the project by setting dates for meetings and having deadlines. This will help you to better manage the group. In the end, you will be holding group members accountable. If that is done right, you have a paper trail to support your leadership skills, and you will "Protect your goal."

Autograph!

Make sure to follow through on all your commitments. Often the person to whom you commit could benefit you in the future.

Have you ever thought of what a signature really represents? It represents a sacred trust. It says that a person has such integrity that they are actually willing to put their name on something of importance.

Our integrity shows in our words and actions. When we say something, we should follow through. Not everyone does so, and some appear to get away with it. However, most employers tend to look at this lack of commitment unfavorably.

What does it mean to give your word to someone? It's a bond, a trust, and an honor; something you can take to the bank even if virtual like so many signatures can be today.

You can count on the fact that you have my word and my commitment to provide you with tools for your job search. I did the best I could for you in this book. Thanks for taking the journey.

Timeout 7.9

Come up with your own slogan to market yourself. What would it be? Keep in mind, "Just do it" has been taken.

I have always used "Play the Game." It helps me approach my life by understanding that there are many rules we need to understand, and it also helps me remember to have fun.

1. What does it mean to give your word to someone?
2. What is your "personal slogan?"
3. Why did you choose this slogan?
4. How does this slogan represent you and in what light?
5. Remember that you must be able to explain this "personal slogan" in an interview.
6. Consider incorporating this slogan on your business card. Again, *uniqueness* matters.

Coach's Tip

I believe in you. If you completed the timeouts, you are on your way to success. Getting experience, the next step, is up to you. Make a promise to yourself to revisit these steps and keep your resume, cover letter, and portfolio fresh and alive.

Please email and tell me what steps worked for you and maybe some new ones you would like to see added. I am always learning.

Sincerely,

Dr. Peter Titlebaum
Peter.Titlebaum@notes.udayton.edu

TIMEOUT HELP FROM REAL LIFE

Timeout 7.3

Performance of Which I'm Proud

I am extremely proud of my performance in completing my Bachelor of Science in Mechanical Engineering. Engineering is a very rigorous academic pursuit that requires intelligence, hard work, and discipline. I think that I rose to the challenge and did quite well. I ended my undergraduate education with a 90% weighted average grade and an honor of distinction for the thesis I wrote.

I intend to improve upon this by completing my MBA with an even higher grade average. While I understand now more than I did when I was an undergraduate that it is more about what you learn than the grade you get, I think that earning good grades is a good goal to set while pursuing academic endeavors.

Risks I Need to Take

The primary risk that I need to take to further my career is to change employers. While I like my current company and appreciate the opportunities they have given me, there are things that they cannot provide that a large, multi-national corporation could. This kind of risk could certainly affect my future. Many large, multi-national companies require their employee to relocate several times while climbing the corporate ladder. My wife and I are very happy with where we live since it puts us close to all of our direct family members. When choosing to work for a large company, we would certainly have to take relocation into serious consideration.

Another crisis that could result in a change of employers could be the fact that large companies often have to cut their workforce when business is bad. At my current employer, job security is very high. If I choose to take the risk and go to work for a large company like P&G, there is a chance I could lose my job. If that happened I would probably give much consideration to returning to Henny Penny. I think that my experience gained from an outside company is the type of perspective that they want and I would then be able to offer it.

Planning, Risk, Crisis, and Evaluation

I will evaluate the risk of moving overseas for a job opportunity. Below are the planning, risk, crisis, and evaluation steps associated:

Planning
- *Finding housing in a foreign city*
- *Establishing transportation*
- *Learning how to speak a foreign language*
- *Furnishing a living space in the new city*
- *Learning the laws of the new location including any tax implications*

Risk
- *The company could decide to close its foreign branches*
- *The company could have corporate layoffs*
- *The new city's cost of living could be dramatically different which could stunt the growth of my retirement funds*
- *The people in the foreign branch of the company could have a negative view of me as an American and thus could fail to work cooperatively with me*
- *My family may not adapt well to the new location*

Crisis
- *My company could go bankrupt*
- *My company could be acquired and the workforce downsized*
- *One of my parents could become ill and require me to take care of him/her*
- *While in a foreign city, US locations could be consolidated leaving no desirable options to which to return*
- *My wife or one of my children could become seriously ill requiring advanced medical procedures that are only readily available in the US*

Evaluation
- *Would this job in a foreign city enhance my ability to climb the corporate ladder?*
- *Would my foreign language skills make me more marketable?*
- *Would the exposure to a different culture be a benefit to my children's long-term success?*
- *Would my decision to move abroad change my early retirement goals?*
- *Would the job in a foreign city lead to an opportunity with a foreign-based company that I would offer even better opportunities?*

What Risk Does My Dream Job Require?

More than likely, my dream job would require me to take a major decrease in salary to get into the field of Baseball Operations. While I'm sure that a General Manager's salary is very nice, I would obviously not start into the field of Baseball Operations with that position. In order to get my foot in the door, I would need to start out at the bottom rung of the corporate ladder. At this point in my life, I cannot see taking that risk. My current position allows my family to live on one salary. I think that a major drop in pay would put an undue amount of stress on my family.

Timeout 7.5

My Comfort Zone

My comfort zone involves working for the same company for nearly twelve years. It involves waiting for management to recognize my leadership and ability and reward me with a managerial promotion. My comfort zone is also accepting whatever pay raise that I am given. It is straying away from interoffice politics because I think they can be dirty. It is keeping a low profile even when I see things differently than senior management does. My comfort zone is socializing with my fellow department members during all employee events rather than getting to know people outside my department.

Three Risks I Can Take

Three risks that I can take to get out of my comfort zone are:

1. *Interview with other companies to see what is out there. While I really like my job and my company, I do not fully know what kind of opportunities await outside of my employer's four walls. Perhaps there is a start-up company full of young, energetic employees that is about to explode. Maybe the grass is greener working for a large, publicly traded company rather than a small, privately*

held company. I will never know until I explore other options.

2. I can try to negotiate a larger raise with my manager. Rather than accepting what is given to me, I could ask for what I think that I am worth. By using salary research and keeping a list of my significant accomplishments, I should be armed with the right tools to win my case. Also, by using data to bolster my case, my manager and I should be able to keep the conversation from focusing on my salary requests and more about what the market commands for the type of position and my contributions.

3. At the next all-employee event, I can choose to sit at a table with people from another department. I could introduce myself and try to put a face (mine) with a name that they may hear or talk to on the phone occasionally. This would also help me to learn who the people are and what their job responsibilities include.

Get Out of Comfort Zone

Another way to get out of my comfort zone would be to more actively participate and network during Product Development and Management Association (PDMA) meetings and conferences. These meetings and conferences are attended by people from some really great, innovative companies including one of my dream employers—Procter and Gamble. I am not enough of an expert on the discipline of Product Management at this point to give a presentation, but when I do feel that I have something to offer, I could present at one of the meetings or conferences. That kind of experience could almost be considered a public interview to everyone in the audience.